INHERITOLATRY

THE FINAL OBSTACLE TO COMPLETING THE GREAT COMMISSION

JAMES D. WISE

Xulon Press

Xulon Press
2301 Lucien Way #415
Maitland, FL 32751
407.339.4217
www.xulonpress.com

Unless otherwise indicated, Scripture quotations taken from the Holy Bible, New International Version (NIV). Copyright © 1973, 1978, 1984, 2011 by Biblica, Inc.™. Used by permission. All rights reserved. Printed in the United States of America.

Edited by Xulon Press.

ISBN-13:9781545603932

TABLE OF CONTENTS

Foreword   Ron Blue vii

Introduction   Finishing the Work xi

Chapter 1   The Prodigal 1

Chapter 2   The Entrepreneur. 7

Chapter 3   The Wanderer 14

Chapter 4   The Inheritance 19

Chapter 5   The Response 23

Chapter 6   The Resources 27

Chapter 7   The Opportunity 34

Chapter 8   The Challenge 43

Chapter 9   The Solution 50

Chapter 10   Inequality is Permitted 58

Chapter 11   Requests are Acceptable 67

Chapter 12   Limitations are Prudent. 76

Chapter 13   Responsibility is Required 86

Chapter 14   The Result 97

FOREWORD

BY RON BLUE

I remember it well. I was rushing through the airport on my way to catch a plane when I spotted a young man who had worked for me many years earlier, Jim Wise. I shouted, "Jim, how are you?" His response was not "Hello," but "You've taught me everything I know about money and money management." I stopped, walked over to where he was standing and said, "Jim I may have given you the basics, but you have taken the basics way beyond anything that I ever dreamed." Jim Wise took content and concepts that I had written about and has applied them at a whole other level of understanding and application. I consider Jim to be a Bible scholar, leader, teacher, counselor, and perhaps most importantly, a practitioner. In other words one who not only thinks deeply about the Biblical principles of money and money management, but who actually gives advice that is fundamentally driven by what God's word has to say about money and money management. His clients and others that he speaks to listen and actually implement what he advises.

I believe, and Jim has documented, that there is more than enough wealth currently in the hands of committed evangelical Christians in the United States to complete the work of the Great Commission. Jim's research sets the number at $5 to $6 trillion that God has entrusted to committed believers and that is expected to be transferred to the next generation before the year 2061. Only a small percentage of these resources would need to be left to kingdom causes – Christian ministers and ministries who God has already strategically placed around the world – in order to complete the work God has called us to. It is not a people issue, but rather a money issue. We have the financial resources to finish the fulfillment of the Great Commission.

My observation over the last 40 years of working with Christians in the area of money management and wealth transfer is that the more wealth someone has the more difficult the wealth transfer decision becomes. Our adult children are unique in their circumstances, and those circumstances can change dramatically over time. This then begs the question for the committed believer: Which biblical principles should guide my decision as to how to best transfer the wealth that God gave me to the next best steward or stewards. Is the next best steward one of my heirs, or might some of God's servants be a better choice?

Jim has done extensive research on what God's word has to say about the topic of inheritance, and he's developed four specific biblical principles to guide us. I believe Inheritolatry is one of those books that will be read and reread by serious financial stewards of God's resources for decades to come. It has the potential to impact literally billions of dollars of wealth being transferred, and maybe more significantly, to help God's people avoid many of the failures and problems associated with the transfer of wealth to a second and third generation.

Jim is a favorite teacher and speaker at Kingdom Advisors, an organization that I helped to found that is committed to training Christians who are financial advisors to apply God's word to the advice that they give. His advice carries authority and authenticity. Fellow professionals listen carefully when he speaks. Jim is an exceptional communicator and you will cherish this book if you are passionate about using the resources entrusted to you by our Lord and Savior Jesus Christ. It is a privilege for me to write the foreword to this book.

INTRODUCTION
FINISHING THE WORK

Five trillion dollars. Not just any five trillion dollars, but five trillion dollars of God's money that has been entrusted to this generation of Christians, presumably for a specific purpose. Five trillion dollars that is currently in the hands of God's people and is well in excess of the amount needed to complete the work of the Great Commission. And the only thing standing between God's money and the completion of God's work is... us.

By "us" I don't just mean we Christians currently stewarding these resources, but also the Christian advisors we've retained to provide counsel with regard to estate planning and wealth transfer. If we hire a non-Christian advisor, we expect to receive secular advice; it would be unreasonable to assume otherwise. When we hire a Christian advisor, however – estate attorney, financial planner, investment advisor, insurance professional, trust officer – it is reasonable to assume we'll be counseled from a biblical perspective. Sadly, such has not been the case, and the result is that our generation is on the verge of squandering those resources God has entrusted to us, so that we might bring to completion the most important task in the history of the world: the Great Commission.

We are living in a truly unique time. As Americans prepare for an unprecedented transfer of wealth to the next generation – a good portion of which is in the hands of evangelical Christians – charitable giving has taken an interesting turn. Even as charitable giving in general is increasing in the United States, giving to the church and faith-based ministries continues to decline (1). Charitable giving among the general population is at record levels, yet many evangelical churches and para-church ministries struggle to raise the support needed to continue their work. Stated another way, while evangelical wealth rapidly rises to record levels, generosity among evangelicals continues to wane.

For many church and ministry leaders, the concern extends well beyond current giving patterns and the budget shortfalls so frequently experienced. Of far greater concern are the prospects for future growth and long-term financial viability. The passing of this excess wealth to a generation that is less generous – and less committed to funding the ongoing work of ministry around the world – is problematic at best. Simply stated, declining generosity presents a challenge not only for the funding of today's ministry work, but also for the work that will need to be done in future generations.

What in the world are we doing with God's money?

While church and ministry leaders might well read the paragraphs above with a mixture of disappointment and frustration, my purpose in making this point is actually to encourage us. I firmly believe the challenge we face in freeing God's resources to fund His work around the world is less the result of Christian greed or ambivalence than of education. What if many of the Christians to whom God has entrusted these excess resources are simply unaware of God's counsel with regard to His intention for their ultimate disposition? What if the primary reason God's people with wealth – and those who advise them – are engaging in estate planning with a secular worldview is because no one has shared with them the biblical perspective on inheritance?

What intrigues me about the level of wealth God has entrusted to this generation of Christians is this: the amount of money is so great that completing the work of the Great Commission can be accomplished with very little change to current financial practices (i.e. giving, saving, lifestyle). How? By simply applying God's principles of inheritance to the estate planning and wealth transfer process.

Learning and obeying God's inheritance principles as they apply to this transfer of wealth can and should result in the completion of the Great Commission in our generation. As you'll see in the coming chapters, God has already provided the resources needed to finish the work, and these resources will be in transition generationally during the next several decades. Discovering and sharing God's inheritance principles is my purpose for writing this book. I want and plan to be among God's people still standing when our part of the work has been completed.

Five trillion dollars, entrusted to God's people to accomplish His work in the world, is coming dangerously close to being diverted to a purpose God did not intend and will not bless. The deep conviction of my heart, and the premise of this book, is as follows:

1. God is the owner of all resources. We are the managers of His resources, and His word provides explicit instruction with regard to His intention for the wealth He entrusts to us.

2. The Great Commission – making disciples of all nations – is a clear and compelling purpose to which God has called His people. Pursuit of this mission is a universal objective for all Christians, transcending denominational lines and doctrinal differences. In this calling there is unity.

3. God has entrusted far more wealth to this generation of Christians than is required to provide for the needs of our families. More important, God has entrusted far more excess wealth to this generation of Christians than is needed to complete our part of the Great Commission.

4. The current wealth transfer plan employed by most Christians is to divide most or all of the estate equally between the adult children. This approach is typically taken without regard to the size of the estate or each adult child's financial need, spiritual commitment or financial responsibility.

5. While many Christians with wealth are very intentional in applying biblical financial principles to the day-to-day

management of their finances, most tend to completely disregard biblical wisdom with regard to the estate planning and wealth transfer process.

6. Ignoring God's perspective with regard to inheritance risks two dangerous outcomes: squandering the resources God has entrusted to our generation to complete the funding of the Great Commission (i.e. being unfaithful stewards), and irreparably damaging the next generation by passing down a significant amount of excess wealth that is either unnecessary or unlikely to be managed in accordance with God's purposes.

Although giving trends in the church can be somewhat discouraging to those of us who long for the completion of the Great Commission and the return of Jesus for His church, I find myself filled with hope and expectation. I absolutely trust in God's sovereign purpose in entrusting such great wealth to this particular generation of His people. We are a blessed and privileged people; our obedience will result in the Gospel being proclaimed to the ends of the earth. We can finish the work.

With these thoughts in mind, let's explore the challenges, opportunities and biblical principles that must be considered in the estate planning and wealth transfer process. But first, a not-so-happy family story that may sound all too familiar.

Chapter 1

The Prodigal

Each sibling fidgeted uncomfortably as they waited for their parents' attorney to join them in the conference room. They were not accustomed to being in the same room together, having lost touch with one another many years ago, and for the most part had little interest in rekindling the relationships. Despite the awkward silence, though, there appeared to be a sense of eager expectation in the faces of at least three of the four siblings. This struck Sarah, the second-born, as particularly unsettling given the reason for their gathering.

Sarah had tried over the years to keep in touch with her brothers and sister, if for no other reason than to honor mom and dad, whose greatest regret in life was watching the family relationships disintegrate and several of their kids wander away from the faith they held so dear. Dad had passed away four months earlier after a prolonged battle with cancer. Mom, having struggled for many years with heart-related health issues, had succumbed to a fatal stroke just a few weeks ago. Their long-time attorney had summoned the four adult children for the reading of the will.

Sarah was the only one of the four children who embraced her parents' faith. She met her husband, Tom, in Bible College, where they committed their lives to serving God wherever His call would lead them. After twenty years in the mission field, Tom and Sarah returned to the U.S. and were currently working with a local ministry providing life skills and job training to the poor in their community. They'd decided to move back home when Sarah's dad became ill, knowing that mom would need help and support in caring for her husband. Despite the pain of losing both parents in such a short period of time, Sarah had considered it a privilege and blessing to help care for mom and dad at the end of their lives.

Tom and Sarah have six children, five biological and a special needs child they adopted while serving overseas. As is the case with many missionary families, finances have always been tight and there is much they've done without. Despite the challenges associated with supporting a family of eight on their relatively meager salaries, though, there was always an admirable sense of contentment in this family. As missionaries, Tom and Sarah were well accustomed to relying on God's provision, and they'd done a great job modeling for their children what it looks like to trust God in all circumstances. As for the kids, they typically didn't ask for things the family couldn't afford or complain about what they didn't have.

Having a special needs child brought challenges as well as abundant blessings. Most of the challenges were financial – the medical bills seemed unending – but God had always faithfully provided and the family's needs were always supplied. As a result, regardless of their income level or living expenses, Tom and Sarah remained committed to tithing, saving and avoiding consumer debt.

Although her mom and dad would surely have been willing to help financially during times when their budget was particularly strained, Tom and Sarah felt it was important to provide for themselves and not become dependent on the generosity of her parents... a perspective clearly not shared by her siblings.

Sarah's oldest brother, Joshua, had chosen a different path. As a young teen he'd been actively involved in church life – youth groups, summer mission trips, playing guitar in the youth worship band – but his participation was more social than spiritual; Josh had never taken Christianity very seriously. He enjoyed mocking Sarah's genuine commitment to following Christ and constantly fought against parental restrictions on how and where he could spend his time. By his junior year in high school, Josh preferred the company of his drinking buddies to the kids at youth group, and he found the "wild girls with no curfew" much more interesting than the Christian gals at church.

By the time he went away to college, Josh had 'graduated' from marijuana to cocaine, and his interest in women – perhaps better described as obsession – eventually led to experimentation with pornography and prostitutes, the latter made possible by the relatively large monthly allowance Josh received during his college years. (His parents didn't want Josh to have to work while attending college; the monthly allowance, they concluded, would enable him to "concentrate fully on his studies.") Josh's life began to spiral out of control as experimentation turned into voluntary addiction, ultimately costing Josh two marriages and a promising career with a prominent pharmaceuticals firm. Since then Josh had bounced around from job to job; finding a new career was difficult given several DUI's and one arrest for cocaine possession.

Tragically, Josh never seemed to learn from his mistakes. On the contrary, he was quite fond of blaming others for his difficult circumstances: his parents' being so strict, he insisted, "pushed me toward the wrong crowd" as a teenager; Sarah's "constant Bible-thumping" pushed him away from church; his former boss' "witch hunt" led to his being fired for illicit drug use. Interestingly, despite Josh's professed atheism and his disdain for Christianity, he occasionally included God in his list of those responsible for "trying to ruin my life."

For many years Josh's parents had tried in vain to restore the broken relationship and get him the help he needed to overcome his addictions. For a while, Mom and Dad were hopeful. Josh would call – seemingly out of the blue – to thank them for not giving up on him. He would give a heartfelt (or well-rehearsed?) "I've learned my lesson" speech and then share the latest plan for getting his life back together. The only help he would need from mom and dad (in addition, of course, to "your continued prayer support") is "some money to help me get back on my feet." When necessary, i.e. if he sensed even the slightest hesitation on his parents' part, Josh would briefly change the subject: "By the way, I found this great new church and I'm thinking about joining the men's Bible study..." Time after time mom and dad would comply, certain that this time Josh was being sincere, only to have their hearts broken anew.

The last time they'd had any contact with Josh, a number of years before their passing, was after they'd made the difficult decision to stop sending money. Both their pastor and attorney had expressed concern that they were enabling Josh, advice they finally heeded. Instead, they pleaded with Josh to come home for a period of time so they could help him to get healthy. Josh became angry, once again blaming them for his problems and cursing their refusal to help. "That's not fair – you guys have all that money and you won't even use some of it to help your own son!" It was this phone conversation, the last they had with Josh, which left them with ongoing feelings of guilt that never quite subsided.

Josh currently lived twenty miles away in one of the more seedy sections of town, working as the day manager of a strip club. To help make ends meet, he'd also been moonlighting as a small-time cocaine dealer. Though his day job doesn't pay very well – just enough money for food, rent and necessities – Josh's evening venture provides the income needed to continue feeding his addictions.

5

As they sat waiting in the conference room, Sarah found herself reminiscing about Josh as a little boy, so full of life and promise. At age ten, Josh had announced his plans to be a pastor when he grew up. By age thirteen, after Josh attended a presentation at church on the human trafficking crisis, he decided instead to become an attorney specializing in human rights. Sarah felt a rush of despair as her thoughts returned to the present. Josh's current ambition, which he's not shy about sharing with anyone who will listen, is to someday have enough money to buy his own strip club.

CHAPTER 2

THE ENTREPRENEUR

I t was Sarah's younger brother, Luke, who had followed somewhat in his dad's footsteps, demonstrating promising business skills from a very early age. Whereas Josh had intentionally strayed from faith and family, ultimately rejecting both, Luke's drift had been much more gradual. It wasn't so much that he didn't love his parents or believe in the God they worshipped, the pursuit of wealth had simply become the greater priority. In time, money and material possessions became Luke's all-consuming passion.

Luke had always viewed his mom and dad as somewhat naive. Though they were certainly caring and involved parents, at times they seemed more concerned with reaching the lost and helping those in need than they were with improving their own standard of living. Luke didn't object to charitable giving, mind you, but giving a minimum of ten percent of their income away seemed excessive, even radical. "Here we are," thought Luke, "still living in the same house and driving used cars, while ten percent of our income is going to people we don't even know. Crazy!"

He never acknowledged it, but several of Luke's most valuable vocational traits seemed to be inherited directly from his dad: a strong work ethic, a passion for quality, and excellent people skills. As teenagers, all four kids had spent summers working in the family business. While each of the kids proved to be responsible and hard working, it was always Luke who came home with new ideas for improving efficiencies, cutting costs and increasing profits.

What began as a wonderful father-and-son relationship, with Luke eager to learn about business and dad enthusiastically training his would-be successor, eventually their differing views of success began to strain the relationship. Luke continued to work summers for his dad through college. Despite presenting his dad with comparative data showing how their supervisors and senior employees were being overpaid by industry standards, and how the company benefits plan was much too generous, dad held fast to the "our-people-are-more-important-than-profits" mantra that had driven Luke crazy for most of his life.

Dad became particularly concerned when Luke, who had always supported his insistence on producing the highest quality products possible, started to bring proposals for cutting corners in the manufacturing process and using lower-cost materials in order to increase profit per unit. Luke also progressed in his fixation on lifestyle, continually expressing his frustration that the family didn't "live like we own a multi-million dollar business."

Once Luke had graduated from college and finished his MBA program, he left the family business to pursue the executive fast track in corporate America. Although from the beginning Luke enjoyed a very attractive compensation package, he tended to always over-extend financially. Lifestyle, in Luke's mind, was a primary gauge of success. He also reasoned that an ever-increasing lifestyle would keep him motivated to perform at the highest level.

Within several years of getting married and starting his family, Luke ran into financial problems. Dad had cautioned him about buying too much too fast, and about the dangers of misusing debt to fund an excessive lifestyle, but his appeal fell on deaf ears. The thirty-five hundred square foot, five-bedroom home they'd just built (for his family of four) was magnificent to behold, but difficult to afford. Luke had felt like a negotiating genius when he convinced the lender to make a 90% loan and then also provide a healthy line of credit for a built-in swimming pool and elaborate Japanese garden landscaping.

In addition to the monthly payments for the large mortgage and home equity line of credit, the financing for two new (and very expensive) cars added $1,500 each month to the family budget. Within a short period of time, so much of Luke's monthly take-home pay was consumed by these loan payments that his wife frequently had to use the credit cards for basic needs such as groceries and clothing. Typically, the family's credit card usage was well beyond what could be paid in full each month, so the balances and minimum monthly payments continued to grow. Despite the mounting pressure from an increasing debt-load and frequent late notices for bills unpaid, Luke's spending patterns never changed. If he saw something he wanted, Luke made the purchase, no questions asked.

Luke's wife had expressed concern on more than one occasion that "we don't need and can't afford all this stuff," but Luke was always confident in his earning ability, and he remained steadfastly committed to enjoying "the abundant life" he'd heard about in church so many years ago. Once his credit lines were maxed-out, expenses exceeded income by a couple thousand dollars each month, and calls from collection agencies had become an almost daily occurrence, Luke finally turned to mom and dad to bail him out. Dad was saddened but not at all surprised by Luke's predicament, and he was very hopeful that Luke had finally learned the painful lesson his dad had sought to help him avoid.

Dad made a loan to Luke with very generous repayment terms, which allowed Luke to pay-off all his credit card debt and one of the car loans. Initially, Luke's spending pattern seemed to change for the better, but he soon returned to his former ways. The car that had just been paid-off, only two years old and still under thirty thousand miles, was traded in for a brand new car. Of course, the price difference after trade-in value was financed, leading back to a second car payment. Luke reasoned that, since they were no longer paying the high credit card interest rates, and the monthly payment on dad's loan was "ridiculously low," the new car payment seemed more than affordable.

Then, several years later, it happened again. Luke was in serious financial straits, and the amount required to bail him out this time was much larger than the first loan (only a small portion of which had as yet been repaid). Still, dad, who often preferred to believe the best about his kids rather than dwelling on demonstrated behavior, convinced himself that Luke was finally ready to be more responsible financially. A second loan was made, incorporating both Luke's new consumer debt burden and the unpaid balance remaining on dad's original loan. Dad's hopeful expectation that Luke was ready to change, however, was quickly replaced by the unpleasant reality.

The evening he stopped by to pick-up the check for this second loan, his parents were stunned by Luke's lack of contrition and what could only be described as a defiant attitude. If he'd been in any way humbled by two significant financial crises, it was certainly not evident. Nor was any gratitude verbalized for mom and dad helping him out again. Instead, rather than taking responsibility for his poor financial decisions, Luke blamed his employer for "refusing to pay me what I'm worth to the company." This problem would be rectified, Luke assured his parents, by "putting some feelers out" to find a job that would recognize his value and pay him properly.

Even more painful than the blatant lack of remorse, though, were several comments that seemed to imply his parents were partly to blame for Luke's financial distress. It should be noted that Luke always made such statements with a wry smile, so it was difficult to tell whether or not he was joking. Still, comments about mom

11

and dad being "so tight with cash" and "giving all that money away when your own kids are in need" – a particularly effective refrain he'd learned from his older brother – always struck a nerve. Upon leaving, Luke also 'joked,' almost under his breath, but loud enough to be heard, "this loan would be even more helpful if it didn't have to be repaid."

Luke's words turned out to be prophetic. The loan from mom and dad would never be repaid. After six months or so, the loan payments once again became erratic. Luke assured his parents that everything was fine – he was just "waiting for my next bonus check to come in." There were sporadic payments for another year, which stopped completely when, inexplicably, Luke moved his family into a larger home. His parents were incredulous. When dad asked how he found a mortgage lender willing to make a large loan to someone with so much debt, Luke flashed a victorious smile: "That's the best part! With the last loan from you and mom I was able to pay-off the car loans and all our credit card debt. My credit is in pretty good shape right now. Most of what I owe is to you, and that doesn't show-up in a credit report!"

Twenty years and two personal bankruptcies later, Luke rarely saw or spoke with his parents in the years leading up to their passing. Not because he was embarrassed to see them – his financial problems, after all, were never of his own making – but because he no longer had much use for them. Like two of his siblings, mom and dad eventually refused to give Luke any more money, no matter how difficult his reported circumstances. Though they'd insisted this was for his own good, Luke was always convinced it was due to their maddening tendency to be so tight with money.

Thumbing through a recent copy of Luxury Travel magazine he'd found in the lobby, Luke impatiently wondered aloud what was taking so long and when the meeting would begin. He'd only blocked an hour and didn't want this meeting to throw off his schedule for the rest of the day. He glanced again at his watch, looked outside to see if their host was on his way, and then turned his attention back to a captivating article reviewing five-star hotels in Morocco.

CHAPTER 3

THE WANDERER

Despite her best efforts to keep in touch over the years, Sarah had very little contact with her younger sister. Although they'd been close and spent a lot of time together as children, the teen years magnified their vast and seemingly irreconcilable differences. Ruth developed an early interest in two areas that Sarah found particularly objectionable: rules violations and parental manipulation. Ruth excelled in appearances: she knew well the type of clothing, friends and language required to convince mom and dad she'd chosen the straight-and-narrow. This charade kept her parents from asking too many questions or checking on her whereabouts, giving Ruth a level of freedom during those years her brother Josh never enjoyed. To those at church, Ruth appeared every bit the committed Christian girl her parents believed her to be. Sarah knew better, but was reluctant to blow the whistle on the sister she was trying so desperately to bring back to Jesus.

Ruth was thirteen years old the first time she snuck out of the house at night, accepting a dare from a boy she'd met at school.

Frequency gradually increased, and Ruth's actions began to attract the attention of other teenage boys. Ruth came to learn that boys in general were just as easy to manipulate as her parents had been, and she thrived on all the attention she was suddenly receiving. Eventually, Ruth developed the habit of disappearing for weekends at a time, with no one knowing where she was or whom she was with. When she'd finally return home, "Stay out of my business!" was the only explanation offered to her frantic parents.

After high school, Ruth tried an out-of-state college for a year, mostly to get away from home. But when the school's "annoying rules" concerning class attendance and GPA cut short her academic career, Ruth decided instead to get a job in retail and move into an apartment with a couple friends from high school. She didn't care to work full-time, so Ruth persuaded her parents to continue the allowance she was receiving during college. "After all, I saved you a lot of money by dropping out."

The next few years were a blur, Ruth navigating her way through a series of different jobs, roommates and boyfriends. Her self-centered disposition and considerable manipulation skills kept her from sustaining any close relationships, which didn't matter to Ruth since she'd always viewed people primarily as a means to an end. A relationship was only worthwhile in Ruth's sight if she was able to benefit from it in some way. If the expected benefits failed to materialize or were of limited duration, Ruth never hesitated in moving on to greener pastures.

No one in the family was surprised when Ruth's first marriage, impulsively entered into after three weeks of dating a guy she'd just met, fell apart before their six-month anniversary... the first of her three divorce proceedings. Rather than lament the failed marriages, however, Ruth actually bragged about how "profitable" marriage had become. "Once I figured out how to do it right."

Sarah had come to understand in time that the marriage 'done right' Ruth was describing had less to do with compatibility and commitment than the financial condition of the chosen husband. After her first marriage, unwittingly entered into with a young man who had no job or money, Ruth shrewdly reasoned that an above-average lifestyle would be more easily attained if she chose more carefully the type of man she would pursue. Since financial gain had become Ruth's objective measure of marital success, each subsequent marriage was considered a significant improvement over the last, with her fourth and current husband by far the most profitable.

The last time Sarah had visited her sister there was an unsettling hardness in Ruth's eyes. Conversation was at first difficult given the infrequent contact and how little they shared in common. Ruth had never expressed any interest in Sarah's life or family, so their initial engagement was limited to small talk. Eventually, though, after her second round of scotch, Ruth began to fill the silence with her thoughts about life, men in general and the drawbacks of being married. By the third round, Ruth began to speak more directly about her own marriage, an uncomfortable discussion that reached its crescendo with Ruth disdainfully mocking the "clueless idiot I married this time."

Sarah was grieved by the condescension in Ruth's voice as she bragged about "how easy it is to get whatever I want." Indeed, Ruth had gotten much, living a lifestyle that many people dream about, but few achieve. When Sarah commented that Ruth's husband seemed like a very nice guy, Ruth smiled distantly, rolled her eyes and noted she wasn't "quite sure how long I'll keep him around. He's only good for paying the bills."

Like Josh, Ruth had long ago lost touch with her parents, and largely for the same reason. Ruth knew her parents had done well financially, so between marriages she would frequently call with a request for money. Ruth was becoming accustomed to enjoying a relatively high standard of living, which she believed to be her parents' responsibility to help her maintain whenever there was no husband in place to do so. The frequent requests for money served to further stress an already strained relationship, and her parent's eventual decision to end such support effectively ended the relationship altogether.

Mom and dad tried numerous times over the years to reconnect with Ruth, but since further financial support was never included in their appeal, Ruth saw no compelling reason to stay in touch. When her dad was first diagnosed with cancer, Ruth had a fleeting thought about visiting her parents. But within a few days, the thought had vanished so completely that, when she later heard from one of her brothers that dad had died, she initially reacted with surprise. Ruth hadn't remembered that dad was sick.

As Ruth stepped-out of the conference room to refresh her coffee, Sarah couldn't help but think about the sweet times they had shared playing together as little girls. Ruth had always been so joyful, so full of life as a child. "Goofy Ruthie," a nickname affectionately given by dad, loved to laugh hysterically and play practical jokes on her family. Her absolute favorite pastime, though, was playing dress-ups, pretending for hours on end to be "Ruthie the Royal Queen," ruling over her devoted make-believe subjects in her expansive make-believe kingdom. Sarah could only smile sadly at the irony.

CHAPTER 4

THE INHERITANCE

"So sorry to keep you all waiting, though I'm glad it gave you some time to reconnect with one another. I'm sure you all have a lot to catch-up on." Forced smiles accompanied the uncomfortable shifting in their seats. Noticing Josh impatiently tapping his finger on the conference table and Luke glancing at his watch, Mr. McNichols assured them, "This won't take too long.

"As you may be aware, your parents appointed me as Executor of their estate. The purpose of today's meeting is to review their will and inform everyone as to how and when their assets will be distributed." This simple introductory statement from the family's long-time attorney seemed to spark a perceptible shift in the mood. Ruth, who'd been mostly staring off into space since she had arrived, set down her coffee mug and became quite focused and attentive. Josh unconsciously moved his chair a bit closer, now leaning in toward Mr. McNichols as if hanging on every word. Poker-faced Luke, never one to allow his facial expression to betray what he was thinking or feeling, appeared to be characteristically unmoved but for a slight, fleeting smile that he quickly suppressed.

Mr. McNichols handed out to each sibling a copy of their parents' estate documents. "These documents are lengthy and somewhat tedious to read – a lot of 'lawyer-speak' – so with your permission I'll summarize what they say. Your parent's estate was valued at just over $8 million dollars as of the date of your mom's death."

Josh most likely didn't intend to verbalize the first thought that came to mind, but he reflexively interrupted with one of his trademark sarcastic comments. "I'll bet their charities would love to get their hands on that money!" Nervous laughter from Luke and Ruth contrasted sharply with Sarah's look of disbelief. Choosing not to be baited into a defense of his clients' charitable practices, Mr. McNichols nonetheless continued by addressing the question Josh unintentionally raised.

"As you know, your mom and dad were committed Christians and among the most generous people I've been blessed to know. They gave liberally to a variety of faith-based causes throughout their lifetime, even back in the old days when the business was just getting started and finances were tight. Although they'd discussed on several occasions their desire to include charitable beneficiaries in their wills, no final decisions were made in that regard prior to your parents' death. As a result, the entire estate will be passed down intact, divided equally between the four of you."

The attorney continued speaking for at least another twenty minutes, most likely well aware that none of his guests heard another word he said. Finally, Josh, unable to wait any longer for an answer to the only remaining question that mattered, once again interrupted Mr. McNichols mid-sentence. "When can we expect this to all happen? I mean, when will all the legal stuff get resolved and everything will be settled?"

Assuming the attorney must not have understood the question since he didn't immediately respond, Josh offered further clarification: "What I'm asking is, when can my brother and sisters expect to get their share of the money?" Somehow it sounded better, at least in Josh's head, to be asking so direct a question on behalf of his siblings rather than himself.

One might have expected the attorney to be taken aback by Josh's directness, but such was not the case. Mr. McNichols was indeed feeling many emotions at this point, but surprise was not one of them. He'd been serving as this family's attorney since before some of the kids were born. He'd had many long, painful discussions with their mom and dad over the years as one-by-one, with the exception of Sarah, the kids turned away, first from their faith and then from their family.

Mr. McNichols had been a consistent and trusted friend, always willing and able to provide a listening ear, biblical wisdom and fervent prayer for the kids. He knew better than anyone the anguish his dear friends experienced as the world successfully seduced, first

Josh, then Ruth, and finally Luke. The sadness he was trying hard to conceal resulted not so much from Josh's inquiry as it did to the hopelessness he felt on behalf of Josh's parents.

It should be noted that the emotions being experienced by several of his guests were quite different from what Mr. McNichols was feeling as he answered Josh's question: the estate should be settled in six months or less. Since their dad had taken steps to sell the family business to several of his managers as soon as he learned of his terminal condition, the only illiquid asset was the family home, which was not expected to take too long to sell. With the most important questions – how much and when – having been answered and no inclination to prolong this family reunion, one by one the siblings began to file out of the conference room.

CHAPTER 5

THE RESPONSE

"Two million bucks!" Josh thought excitedly to himself; the voice in his head so loud that he wondered for a moment if his words could be heard. "Christmas came early this year!" Josh's imagination raced gleefully, as he contemplated the most productive allocation of his newfound wealth. A nicer apartment was certainly in order, and buying a strip club was a no-brainer. "I'm tired of working for someone else," he thought; but the first order of business, Josh decided, was to celebrate his good fortune. His modest income had forced him to settle for a much lower grade of cocaine than he'd been able to enjoy back when there were no bills consuming his generous college allowance. "No more settling for second best," Josh affirmed, as he walked back to his car with a confident look on his face and a bounce in his step that hadn't existed for many years.

Ruth was unusually animated as she quickly left the meeting. Neglecting to acknowledge anyone upon departing, Ruth immediately started planning for "life without the idiot". Marriage might indeed have been profitable, but it was far too demanding and restrictive for Ruth's taste. At long last, she would be in a position to enjoy life on her own; free from the annoyances and expectations that invariably accompanied the financial security her marriages provided. As the elevator approached the lobby, Ruth couldn't help but chuckle when a related serendipity crossed her mind: as an added bonus for the dissolution of marriage number four, Ruth would likely retain half of all their jointly owned property in addition to the generous inheritance she would soon receive. Oblivious to the folks around her as she exited the elevator, Ruth couldn't help but utter aloud the first words of gratitude she'd been able to manage in over twenty-five years: "Thanks Mom and Dad!"

Luke was the last to leave, an interesting development, given his earlier complaint about having limited time available for this meeting. Not surprisingly, Luke was the only sibling with an interest in such matters, as the deadline for filing the estate tax return, possible advantages of using the Alternate Valuation Date, and whether any "creative loopholes" were available to avoid paying estate taxes. He was visibly pleased when Mr. McNichols explained that creative loopholes were unnecessary; the total value of estate assets and the planning Luke's parents had done ensured that their estate would pass entirely estate tax-free.

Satisfied with the attorney's responses to all of his inquiries, Luke's tone quickly shifted from negotiator to politician. He proffered, on behalf of himself and his siblings, "heart-felt appreciation" for all that Mr. McNichols had done for their parents over the years.

Luke's oft-practiced and polished delivery of insincere praise had become one of his more valuable business skills. His lack of genuineness would likely have gone undetected by a less discerning attorney; one who didn't know Luke so well.

As he left the building, Luke immediately called his wife to inform her that the new beach house he'd had his eye on was about to become a reality. "I told you I'd figure out a way to get it! I'm the only executive in my division who doesn't have a vacation home." Luke became animated – and quite annoyed – when his wife dared suggest they consider using the inheritance to repay the mounting debt load, maybe even pay-off their mortgage. In frustration, Luke cut the call short, wondering once again if his "ultra-conservative wife will ever loosen up and learn how to enjoy life."

Sitting in their car, Tom held his sobbing wife, uncertain as to which source of pain was greater: the loss of her beloved parents or the life choices of her siblings. Sarah whispered through her tears, "I miss mom and dad." Tom didn't need to remind her that she would see her parents again, the next time in a place where there would be no more sorrow or death, a place where God would wipe away every tear.

They sat in silence for another ten minutes or so before Sarah spoke again. "At least we can continue mom and dad's generous legacy by investing most of our inheritance in God's work." Her deep sadness was temporarily soothed by their ensuing conversation about the many ministries they could bless in her parents' name and the number of lives that could be eternally impacted for Christ. Sarah probably didn't notice the look of admiration in Tom's eyes as he considered what a godly woman she was and how blessed he was to be her husband. "She's so much like her mom and dad," Tom thought to himself as they drove away.

Long after the siblings had left Mr. McNichols remained in his seat, alone in the conference room. He was deep in thought, a troubled look on his weary face. He couldn't help wondering if he should have counseled his clients differently. Why had it not occurred, either to him or to his clients, that the common practice of dividing the estate equally among the kids might do more harm than good? He hoped he hadn't indirectly contributed to the wrecked lives he feared would result from the pending inheritance.

CHAPTER 6

THE RESOURCES

I suppose every generation of Christians has longed to be the last, to be eyewitnesses to the triumphant return of Christ our King. To that end, the Christian church throughout the ages – since first given her marching orders by Jesus Himself (Mt 28:18-20, Acts 1:8) – has united around the mission He assigned to us: proclaiming the Gospel to the ends of the earth and making disciples of all nations as we patiently await His return.

> *And this gospel of the kingdom will be preached in the whole world, as a testimony to all nations, and then the end will come.* (Mt 24:14)

Still, it is not uncommon for evangelical churches and ministries obediently participating in this life-transforming, world-changing mission to share a common frustration: pursuit of a godly vision that seems far greater than the resources available to fund it. Why is this? Assuming the vision derives from leadership's prayerful consideration of God's word and commands, a lack of funding to pursue the vision can only be attributed to one of two causes. Either God lacks the resources needed to complete the work He has assigned to His people, or those resources God has provided for the completion of this work are not being used for His intended purpose. Let's consider God's perspective with regard to both options.

Is God Lacking the Necessary Resources?

A brief survey of some familiar Bible passages will help us answer this important question. How does God's word address the issue of whether or not He has at His disposal the resources that are needed to complete the work of making disciples of all nations?

To the Lord your God belong the heavens, even the highest heavens, the earth and everything in it. (Dt 10:14)

Yours, Lord, is the greatness and the power and the glory and the majesty and the splendor, for everything in heaven and earth is yours. Yours, Lord, is the kingdom; you are exalted as head over all. Wealth and honor come from you; you are the ruler of all things. (1 Chr 29:11-12a)

Who has a claim against me that I must pay? Everything under heaven belongs to me. (Job 41:11)

The earth is the Lord's and everything in it, the world and all who live in it. (Ps 24:1)

I have no need of a bull from your stall or of goats from your pens, for every animal of the forest is mine, and the cattle on a thousand hills. I know every bird in the mountains, and the insects in the fields are mine. If I were hungry I would not tell you, for the world is mine, and all that is in it. (Ps 50:10-12)

For the Lord is the great God, the great King above all gods. In his hand are the depths of the earth, and the mountain peaks belong to him. The sea is his, for he made it, and his hands formed the dry land. (Ps 95:3-5)

"The silver is mine and the gold is mine," declares the Lord Almighty. (Hag 2:8)

God is not lacking in financial resources because all of the resources in the world belong to Him. Whatever amount of money is needed to complete the work of the Great Commission (Mt 28:18-20), we can rest assured that God has at His disposal the funds necessary to finish the work. God owns absolutely everything.

What, then, is our role with regard to the money and possessions God has entrusted to us? We are simply stewards, or managers, of His resources (Mt 25:14-30). God has given us the responsibility to manage His wealth in accordance with His instructions, regardless of the amount or period of time He has sovereignly determined to entrust it to our care.

Since the Bible makes clear that the problem is not a lack of resources on God's part, we must seriously consider the second option, namely that those resources God has provided to His people for the completion of this work are not being used for His intended purpose.

Are We Faithfully Managing His Resources?

Assessing personal faithfulness with regard to the management of God's resources is the responsibility of every Christian individually. It is difficult to draw general conclusions about our collective success – or lack thereof – as the people of God with regard to biblical stewardship. God's word, however, is decidedly cautious about our attitude toward His money and our flesh's inclination toward the pursuit and accumulation of earthly possessions.

Whoever loves money never has enough; whoever loves wealth is never satisfied with their income. This too is meaningless. (Ecc 5:10)

Then he said to them, "Watch out! Be on your guard against all kinds of greed; life does not consist in an abundance of possessions." (Lk 12:15)

No one can serve two masters. Either you will hate the one and love the other, or you will be devoted to the one and despise the other. You cannot serve both God and money. (Mt 6:24)

Those who want to get rich fall into temptation and a trap and into many foolish and harmful desires that plunge people into ruin and destruction. For the love of money is a root of all kinds of evil. Some people, eager for money, have wandered from the faith and pierced themselves with many griefs. (1 Tim 6:9-10)

Now listen, you rich people, weep and wail because of the misery that is coming on you. Your wealth has rotted, and moths have eaten your clothes. Your gold and silver are corroded. Their corrosion will testify

31

against you and eat your flesh like fire. You have hoarded wealth in the last days. (Jas 5:1-3)

Do not love the world or anything in the world. If anyone loves the world, love for the Father is not in them. For everything in the world—the lust of the flesh, the lust of the eyes, and the pride of life—comes not from the Father but from the world. (1 John 2:15-16).

The choice is clear: We can love and worship God or we can love and worship His money. In the Spirit, we long to become more like Jesus and to use the resources entrusted to us for His glory and His purposes. In the flesh, however, we are prone to prefer the things of this world. We begin to live as if God's money is actually ours, more money is always better and contentment comes from wealth rather than from God. We find ourselves hoarding God's wealth for our own purposes, seeking financial independence not only for ourselves, but also for future generations. When this happens, we are in jeopardy of squandering those resources God has entrusted us to complete the work He has assigned to us.

Is it possible that God, in His infinite wisdom and sovereign purpose, has entrusted to this generation of Christians <u>all</u> of the resources needed to complete the Great Commission? Further, is it possible that we are – consciously or unconsciously – stockpiling these resources for another purpose entirely? Are we continuing to accumulate and store-up God's wealth with the intention of passing it all down to the next generation rather than releasing some or most for Kingdom use? If so, can we say with confidence that we believe this was God's intended purpose for the excess wealth He has entrusted to our care – to make the next generation so wealthy that they have no need of God (Rev 3:17)?

Few would dispute the notion that we represent the wealthiest generation of Christians in the history of the church. As we'll see in the coming chapters, God has entrusted an unprecedented amount of wealth to His people in our generation, wealth that is well in excess of what will ever be needed or consumed in our lifetime. If, indeed, evangelical churches and para-church ministries are lacking the resources needed to do the work God has invited and commanded His people to do, what conclusion must we draw with regard to our faithfulness in managing the wealth He has so graciously entrusted to us?

Faithfulness in all things is measured by conformity to God's word: His stated purposes and commands. In order for each of us to assess the degree to which we're being faithful, both in our day-to-day management of His resources and our estate and wealth transfer plans, we must first understand God's perspective. That is our ultimate destination, to discover and apply God's wisdom with regard to inheritance.

The next few chapters will explore the opportunity, the challenge and the principles we'll need to be aware of in our quest to faithfully navigate the wealth transfer process.

Chapter 7

The Opportunity

I suggested in the previous chapter the likelihood that every generation of Christians has hoped for the return of Jesus in their lifetime. While I believe this is equally true of the church in our day, there is one significant difference between prior generations and ours: it is to us that God has entrusted the resources needed to finish the work. Whether we prove ourselves faithful or unfaithful in our stewardship of these resources, we'll never be able to stand before Jesus and give the excuse that we didn't finish the work because we didn't have enough money. This is both the opportunity we're presented with and the responsibility for which we'll be held accountable.

Unprecedented Wealth Transfer

How much money are we talking about? If you've read any books or articles discussing the vast amount of wealth to be transferred during the next 30-50 years, you've probably seen figures ranging between $40 trillion and $120 trillion. For purposes of this book I'm relying on a research report entitled *A Golden Age of Philanthropy Still Beckons: National Wealth Transfer and Potential for Philanthropy Technical Report* by John J. Havens and Paul G. Schervish (Center on Wealth and Philanthropy Boston College, Released May 28, 2014). The amount of wealth to be transferred between now and 2061, assuming an average 2% growth rate and continuation of the current estate tax exemption, is approximately $67 trillion (Table 5A, page 68). Should we experience a higher growth rate over the next 45 years, this amount could increase to well in excess of $100 trillion.

But how much of this wealth is in the hands of God's people? For that answer we turn to another source.

Wealth Entrusted to Evangelical Christians

In his excellent book, The Great Evangelical Recession (1) – a must-read for church and ministry leaders, as well as Christians with excess wealth – John Dickerson discusses the current state of evangelicalism in America. In reviewing the results of four independent research studies that assess the part of our population who identify as committed followers of Jesus Christ, Dickerson concludes:

> Let's now look at four nationally recognized specialists, each with differing credentials, differing motivations, and differing research methodologies. Separately, all four researchers have found that

35

evangelicals account for 7 to 8.9 percent of the United States population. (2)

While these figures might be much lower than what you've seen in the past, these researchers were looking beyond those who simply call themselves Christians or identify as "born again," to focus on those who actually believe what evangelicals have historically believed. As most of us who follow Jesus have observed, there is a vast difference between the person who identifies as a Christian because they 'walked the aisle and prayed the prayer' and one who identifies Jesus Christ as Lord of his or her life and God's word as divinely inspired and inerrant.

How, then did I arrive at the $5 trillion figure mentioned in the Introduction? If we multiply the total amount of wealth to be transferred ($67 trillion) by the portion of the population identifying as committed evangelical Christians (7.0% to 8.9%), we arrive at a range of $4.7 to $5.9 trillion. Thus my conclusion that, of the $67 trillion that will change hands between now and 2061, approximately $5 trillion is in the hands of God's people. And lest we forget, it is His money, not ours.

How Much to Finish the Work?

This leads to the most important question, the one that is by far the most difficult to quantify. How much money will be needed to complete our part of the Great Commission?

I should probably note that by highlighting "our part" I'm simply acknowledging the primacy of the Holy Spirit's role in both conversion (John 3:8, 16:8-11) and sanctification (Rom 15:16, 2 Thes 2:13), and the fact that God alone has determined the timing of Jesus' return (Mt 24:36, Acts 1:7). We are blessed to participate in this glorious work of making disciples, but we can only accomplish, and will only be held accountable for, our part of the process. Absent the work of the Holy Spirit, our best efforts will be fruitless.

So, how much money will be needed to finish our part of the work? The answer depends on how we quantify the process of making disciples of people from every nation, tribe and language. I've given this a lot of thought and concluded that, at a minimum, there are two parts to this process. First, the evangelical church needs to have a missionary and/or church planting presence among every remaining unreached people group. The first step in the discipleship process is the proclamation of the Gospel of Jesus Christ.

> *Everyone who calls on the name of the Lord will be saved. How, then, can they call on the one they have not believed in? And how can they believe in the one of whom they have not heard? And how can they hear without someone preaching to them? And how can anyone preach unless they are sent? As it is written: How beautiful are the feet of those who bring good news!* (Rom 10:13-15)

Second, it is vitally important that every people group in the world has access to the Bible in their own heart language. Faith still comes from hearing and hearing by the word of God (Rom 10:17). The Bible is an indispensable part of the disciple-making process, and for that reason I firmly believe that a key part of the Great Commission includes Bible translation. Consider the initial launch of the church at Pentecost. What was the Holy Spirit's first order of business as He prepared the hearts of the people to hear and respond to Peter's proclamation of the Gospel? He first made sure everyone present heard the disciples declaring the wonders of God *"in their own languages"* (Acts 2:11, emphasis mine). It is not possible to overstate the importance of God's written word in the process of making disciples. If we're to successfully make disciples of all nations, we must provide God's written word to all nations.

Quantifying the cost of the second objective is less complicated than the first. Wycliffe Bible Translators, when launching the Last Languages Campaign in 2008, set as their objective to begin translating the final group of languages by 2025. The estimated cost? One billion dollars. (That's billion – with a "B" – as opposed to the trillions we've been discussing.) As of this writing there remain approximately 1,700 languages that have no portion of God's word in written form. Assuming the last languages begin being translated in 2025, it is reasonable to conclude the Bible translation part of the Great Commission can be accomplished in our lifetime as long as the resources needed to fund this work are provided.

What about the first objective? How much will it cost to send a missionary presence or church planting team to every remaining unengaged people group? Let's begin by trying to identify the number of people groups in the world that have yet to be reached with the Gospel. Consider the following:

> Data from the International Mission Board (IMB) of the Southern Baptist Convention, the largest denominational mission board in the world, suggests that there are over 3,000 ethnic people groups that are not only unreached, but also completely unengaged, meaning there is no known active, on-site church planting effort underway and few if any known believers. To say that a people group is unengaged means there are definitely no missionaries, in all likelihood no outreach, no church or fellowship of believers, no Christian materials, and few if any Bibles in these people groups. (3)

Although a larger number of people groups (approx. 9,500 according to Joshua Project) can be classified as either unreached, formerly or falsely reached, or minimally reached, more than two-thirds have at least a modest evangelical presence represented among them. What about the cost to reach the one-third of these people groups that is completely unengaged?

Let' assume the annual cost of sending a missionary family or team from a sponsoring agency in North America is $75,000 per year (4). Of course, the cost would be greatly reduced if the sending agency was indigenous and the missionary team was native, but that scenario is highly unlikely with an unengaged people group (vs. unreached people group that already has at least a modest Christian presence).

If the resources were given today in support of this work and the missionaries or church planting teams were available to be sent, it would cost less than $5 billion to support 3,000 teams (one per unengaged people group) for the next twenty years.

What Does It All Mean?

I should point out that my focus here is not mathematical precision – some languages will cost more than others to translate and some unengaged people groups will cost more than others to reach – but rather to get a general idea of how much it will cost to bring God's written word, along with an evangelical missionary or church planting presence, to every people group in the world. Disciples are to be made in all nations, so this seems like a reasonable approach to quantifying the cost of finishing the work.

Assuming you agree that we're at least in the ballpark in terms of identifying the specific work that needs to be done and how I've gone about estimating the cost, the sum total of these two disciple-making projects is around $6 billion dollars. Not to be redundant, but that's billion with a "B." Perhaps we want to be more aggressive in the number of missionaries sent out and the number of people groups reached. Doubling the size of these teams increases the cost to less than $11 billion. Sending two of these larger teams (instead of one) to each people group will cost less than $21 billion. Multiplying the effort by sending two additional teams to the other two-thirds of people groups with a limited witness for Christ (less than 2% of the population being evangelical Christians) will cost less than $61 billion. As you can see, even the most aggressive effort to make disciples of every nation will scarcely put a financial dent in the vast amount of wealth God has entrusted to this generation of Christians in the U.S.

Given the level of financial resources currently in the hands of God's people, the objective of making disciples among every nation, tribe and language would appear to be well within reach. And yet it's not. Why? Because, for the most part, our collective wealth transfer plan is to take the $5 trillion (with a "T") God has entrusted to us and divide it equally between our kids. Without regard to their financial need, spiritual commitment or financial responsibility. Without regard to the damage that will surely be done when the next generation is handed enough money to stop working, start playing, and indulge any worldly desire their sinful flesh might be attracted to. And most frightening, without regard to Who this money belongs to and the purpose for which He entrusted it to us.

But it's not too late. As noted earlier, I believe the reason for the current state of evangelical estate planning is more likely rooted in a lack of education than inherent greed or irresponsibility. Most Christians, given a clear understanding of God's instructions, are more likely than not to choose obedience. That said, with every opportunity comes a challenge, and the challenge we face in the wealth transfer process is formidable because it is deceptively subtle and often unrecognizable. Now that we've identified the incredible opportunity God has given us to finish the work, let's turn our attention to exploring this unseen challenge.

CHAPTER 8

THE CHALLENGE

Friends who have struggled with alcoholism will often share that the first step in overcoming this addiction was to acknowledge the problem. One of Satan's most effective weapons is to convince us that we don't really have a problem – we are in complete control of our behavior. The beginning of our healing process is acknowledging the truth and naming our sin struggle. It is much easier to battle an enemy that has been clearly identified, one that we are consciously aware of. Identifying the enemy is what I hope to accomplish in this chapter.

Inheritance Trends

In my thirty-plus years of providing financial counsel and reviewing estate documents, I can count on one hand (a couple of fingers, to be more specific), the number of estates that did something other than dividing the money equally between the kids. Even though some Christian families have incorporated charitable giving into their estate documents (far fewer estates and far less money than you might imagine), still the remainder of these assets, and the larger share by a significant margin, are to pass to the kids equally. Some folks have restricted the age at which the kids receive full control of their inheritance, the age usually ranging between 21 and 35 with portions of the inheritance distributed along the way. But the result is the same regardless of the timing: the vast majority of these excess resources – in most cases 100% – passes directly to the next generation, whether the estate value is $500 thousand, $5 million, $50 million or more.

Suffice it to say, the next generation has been provided with much more of an incentive to dwell on the passing of their parents than on the return of Jesus Christ.

On the surface, this might not seem like much of a concern, especially to folks whose adult kids are walking with the Lord. Some of our adult kids love Jesus, support churches and evangelical ministries, and manage money reasonably well. What's the problem with responsible kids receiving an inheritance, even a large inheritance? The most obvious answer is that the money is not ours to give away. God is the owner, yet it seems that the majority of our estate planning decisions are being made without consulting Him as to His intended use of these resources. Just because we *can* pass a large estate down to our kids doesn't mean that we *should*. Just because our kids are responsible with money doesn't mean we should indiscriminately increase their wealth. It's God's money, so it should be God's decision.

The second reason it might be problematic to leave a large inheritance, even to adult kids who are walking with the Lord, is that both charitable giving practices and commitment to Christ's church are in rapid decline among evangelical Christians in the next generation. Giving to the Lord's work is becoming an after-thought. Let's first look at the statistics and then consider the implications.

Giving Trends

Generational giving trends among evangelical families are not particularly encouraging. According to the research results reported in The Great Evangelical Recession (1):

- Giving on the whole among evangelicals has been decreasing for years.
- Evangelical donations are on course to drop by 70% within 25-30 years.
- Each ensuing generation in the church is increasingly "unreliable, unpredictable, and less generous" than the previous generation.

It will not surprise us baby-boomer Christians to learn that our parents' generation was decidedly more generous than we are. We baby-boomers have managed to straddle well the fence between materialism and generosity. But research shows that the next generation is less generous still, exceeded only in their lack of generosity by the generation that follows. (2)

In other words, if nothing changes, the resources available for Kingdom work will continue to decline, eventually making it difficult for many churches and evangelical ministries to keep their doors open. Do we think that pouring more money out on the next generation will reverse this trend? Is it reasonable to assume that adult Christians who already have more regard for lifestyle than mission will suddenly discover a generosity gene once made independently wealthy through inheritance? History and experience would suggest otherwise.

Another, perhaps more troubling (though understandable) pattern emerging among the next generation of Christians is a decided distrust of the two primary institutions God has raised up to make disciples: the church and para-church ministries. Those of us actively engaged in discipling the next generation can attest to this fact even without reviewing the research. It makes sense, doesn't it? How many highly publicized scandals have this generation witnessed among church and ministry leaders? How many reports of financial impropriety or moral failure have they grown up observing in religious institutions? These tabloid headlines have done little to promote the next generations' confidence in the people and organizations that exist to do God's work in the world.

As a result, even in cases where the next generation is sufficiently moved by the Spirit to give money to charitable causes, they might be much more likely to give to individuals in need – or even secular humanitarian causes – than to churches and evangelical ministries. And while I very much appreciate all non-profits that are serving those in need, I must recognize their necessary limitations. Daily bread given to the hungry that is not accompanied by an introduction to the Bread of Life is of limited value. Such bread can only bring temporary relief from a physical ailment, never permanent relief from a much more serious spiritual ailment. Evangelical churches and ministries, flawed as many may be, are the engine driving the Great Commission. Evangelical giving is the fuel powering that engine, and the supply of fuel is rapidly decreasing.

Herein lies the spiritual and practical conflict. God has entrusted a significant amount of His money to this generation of evangelical Christians, along with written instructions as to His intended purpose for it. The amount we've been given to manage is well above what will be needed to complete the work He has assigned to us. Our generation, however, continues to accumulate rather than distribute, and our estate documents ensure the eventual transfer of this wealth to the next generation, a generation that has demonstrated considerably less interest in generosity, church and mission. Disconcerting thought? It is for me, and I hope it's becoming so for you.

For most of us, unless we are prepared to make some changes, this is the estate plan we'll have to stand before Jesus and try to explain. At this point, you might be wondering how we got here. How is it that Christians of our generation who have intentionally embraced God's ownership and joyfully practiced biblical steward-ship, have estate plans that fail to reflect these same convictions? How is it that we have written estate documents in place that will, at best, greatly reduce the funds available for Kingdom work, and at worst, damage or destroy the next generation?

The Enemy: Inheritolatry

I've given this issue much thought and prayerful consideration over the past few years and here is what I've concluded: the subtle and unseen enemy we've succumbed to is Inheritolatry. This is, of course, not a real word, but one I created to help us understand what we're dealing with. Simply stated, Inheritolatry is the idolatry of inheritance. What's interesting about this particular form of idolatry is that it is often passed down to our adult kids long before the money they'll inherit.

Some of us might at first object to the thought of inheritance being an idol, at least for the generation leaving it. After all, isn't it good – even biblical – to leave our kids and grandkids an inheritance? It certainly can be. Proverbs 13:22a teaches, *A good person leaves an inheritance for their children's children.* But should we deduce from this proverb that passing down large amounts of God's wealth to the next generation without regard to financial need, spiritual commitment and financial responsibility is what He had in mind? As you'll see in the chapters that follow, such an interpretation is in direct conflict with the whole counsel of Scripture regarding inheritance.

The issue is not whether those of us with excess resources should be willing to leave an inheritance. Leaving an inheritance is fine and can certainly be a blessing to our heirs. The more pressing issue is, how much of an inheritance should we leave? What portion of those excess resources that God has entrusted to us should be passed down to our kids and how much does He want invested in the Great Commission? To the extent we've become more concerned with how much we can leave to the kids than how much we can give to the Kingdom, it is likely we're giving in to Inheritolatry at some level. And I can assure us that once we've become seduced by Inheritolatry, our adult kids will quickly follow. Definitely not the legacy we want to leave.

Let's look at this enemy in greater detail and then discuss the biblical principles that will bring victory over it.

CHAPTER 9

THE SOLUTION

As we prepare to address the biblical inheritance principles we can use in designing our wealth transfer plans, let's take a closer look at how Inheritolatry manifests itself and how we can recognize it in our families. I'll begin by proposing a more precise definition of the term, both as it applies to us and to our heirs.

Defining "Inheritolatry"

For Christian parents, Inheritolatry is the determination to leave significant financial resources to our adult children without regard to financial need, spiritual commitment, financial responsibility or size of the estate. This is our default, incidentally – what I call the American Way of estate planning. Most Christian parents consider it "unfair" to do otherwise, and many Christian advisors, unfortunately, reinforce this notion. In both cases, there is a complete disregard for God's ownership and God's principles for inheritance.

For adult children, Inheritolatry is the unhealthy fixation on funds and property to be inherited, often characterized by a highly consumptive lifestyle and sense of material entitlement. Sometimes we parents are prone to denial with regard to our adult kids struggling with Inheritolatry. We'll often disregard the constant demands for more money and the attitude that conveys, "The money is just as much mine as yours" because denial is a bit less painful than acknowledging what our wealth has done to our kids. However, there's nothing to be gained from denial. While these characteristics are certainly unpleasant for Christian parents to observe and acknowledge, they are unmistakable even to the casual observer. As we've discussed, identifying and naming the sin is the first step in the healing process.

Now that we've reviewed the definitions, let's discuss how to diagnose this condition. Over the years I've observed two different types of behavior in Christian parents that signal a hidden struggle with Inheritolatry: practical and verbal indicators. As you review the following caution signs, ask yourself whether one or more might apply to you or your spouse.

Verbal Indicators of Inheritolatry

Those unknowingly struggling with Inheritolatry will often make comments similar to these:

- "I want my kids to have it easier than I did."

- "I want my kids to enjoy all the things I never had as a child."
- "I suppose it's true that we've spoiled our children."
- "I can't allow my children to live below the standard of living they've become accustomed to."
- "My primary estate planning goal is to make sure my kids are well provided for."

Sound familiar? Whether or not these words have escaped our own mouths, we've almost certainly heard them from others. These parental objectives, spoken or unspoken, often result in less-than-desirable financial attitudes among the adult kids: entitlement, materialism and ingratitude to name a few.

Unlike many of us, most of our children have been raised in upper middle class homes and have enjoyed some privileges we might not have had as children. Large homes, new cars, nice clothes, private school, perhaps a vacation home... for many of our kids this became the norm. Unfortunately, the lifestyle our kids became accustomed to as children quickly became the lifestyle they expected – even demanded – in adulthood. Is it possible that we unconsciously fed this expectation?

Most in my parents' generation, and many in mine, started out with very little and worked diligently to provide for our families. We remember fondly the times our date night consisted of a store-bought package of cupcakes, eaten on a checkered tablecloth spread on the living room floor of our apartment, because we couldn't afford to go out. We smile as we reminisce about eating spaghetti five nights a week because money was tight and pasta was cheap. Some of our most precious and memorable 'God stories' occurred during times when we didn't know where the money would come from to pay the rent or feed the kids. Those of us with such stories wouldn't trade them for anything. And yet, many of us have committed our lives to making sure our kids never get to enjoy the same experiences.

Practical Indicators of Inheritolatry

Some of us have learned to be prudent with our speech – we're much more inclined to keep our deep thoughts and motivations to ourselves or share them only with those we trust most. I'm one of these people. Though we may be able to relate to some of the verbal indicators of Inheritolatry, it is possible that none of these statements ever escaped our lips. Not that we didn't think these thoughts, mind you, we're just too guarded in our speech to let anyone other than our closest confidants know what we're thinking.

For those who aren't as keen on verbalizing our thoughts and attitudes, how can we assess our Inheritolatrous (another word I made up, but hopefully you get the point) tendencies? This one, thankfully, is easier to discern. There are a couple of unmistakable behaviors that likely point to our willing submission to Inheritolatry:

* You are planning to pass down an equal share of your estate to one or more adult children with a demonstrated history of:

  - poor financial decisions
  - irresponsible spending patterns
  - addictive or destructive behavioral patterns
  - estrangement from parents, broken relationships
  - a sense of entitlement
  - abandoning/rejecting the Christian faith

* You have not designed your estate transfer plan using the same biblical stewardship principles you've been applying to the management of your day-to-day finances.

I feel a great burden for those readers who experienced a sense of pain and anguish as you recognized your adult children in the points made above. I'm praying for you as I write these words. My purpose is not to cause pain, but rather to bring encouragement, biblical encouragement. God alone can explain how three kids can be raised in the exact same Christian environment and one can go badly astray. How one can be a leader in youth group and fervent evangelist as a teen, and then abandon the faith completely during the college years. We've all experienced it, either in our own family or one we're close to. While few things are more difficult to discuss than an adult child struggling with addiction, estrangement or abandonment of the faith, it is a reality we cannot ignore. Because it's God's money we're dealing with, and passing a significant amount of His money to adult kids in this situation is far more likely to destroy their lives than save them.

Biblical Wisdom

One of the greatest joys I have in my vocation is helping Christians manage their finances and estates in accordance with biblical principles. I can't imagine a work that is more life-giving and fulfilling. The precious folks I get to serve are contributing countless millions of dollars each year to advance the Gospel, make disciples of Jesus Christ, and serve people in His name around the world. What is the most challenging financial decision many of these committed Christ-followers face with regard to faithfully managing His resources? The estate planning and wealth transfer process. Why? Because, unlike the biblical principles of financial planning that are easily discerned from Scripture and commonly taught, the biblical principles of estate planning are a bit more elusive.

It might be helpful to share the process I went through in discovering God's principles for inheritance. I began with a word search – "inherit" and "inheritance" – and copied every verse in the Bible that mentioned either word. Then I began to study each verse and look for concepts that clearly applied to the wealth transfer process. Those familiar with God's word will not be surprised to know that most of the New Testament references to inheritance refer, not to money or possessions, but our inheritance in Christ. While I cherish and rejoice in this truth, these passages did not lend themselves to understanding God's perspective on wealth transfer.

The Old Testament passages, however, were extremely helpful and valuable for this purpose. By and large, the O.T. passages dealing with inheritance focused mostly on the land God set aside for His people. By studying the biblical teaching surrounding Israel's land inheritance – the primary estate assets initially controlled by God's people in the O.T. – we can learn a great deal about how God would have us steward the money, land and possessions He has entrusted to us in our generation. This biblical wisdom is invaluable as we plan for the eventual transfer of the wealth He has entrusted to us.

The Solution

What is the solution to our Inheritolatry dilemma? How can God's people break the bondage of secular thinking with regard to our estate planning and ensure that we are seeking God's wisdom before deciding on the ultimate disposition of our estates? As with any struggle we might face, the solution is to discover, embrace and implement the principles laid out in God's word.

The four primary biblical wealth transfer principles are as follows:

1. Inequality is permitted
2. Requests are acceptable
3. Limitations are prudent
4. Responsibility is required

Each of the next four chapters will look at one of these principles in detail, including a review of the supporting Scripture, the practical application and some helpful examples.

Chapter 10

Inequality is Permitted

"It's not fair!" This is the heart's cry of a generation of entitled, upper middle class Americans. It starts early. Sometime between our toddlers uttering their first words and their learning to string together a relatively coherent full sentence, this phrase invariably enters their underdeveloped vocabulary. Withholding a toy or treat they have their eye on? "It's not fair!" Administering discipline for their undesirable behavior? "That's not fair!" A sibling gets to play with their new birthday present while the toddler is left with only 'used' toys? Definitely "Not fair!"

Thankfully, the toddler phase is short-lived and this attitude is quickly replaced by selflessness and the desire to put others first... or is it? Unfortunately, this sinful nature-induced attitude remains, both with our kids and, if we're honest, with us as well. A common aspect of our fallen nature is that we resist authority and prefer to determine for ourselves what is right or wrong, fair or unfair. As with Adam and Eve in the garden, we might highly esteem God's instructions until they come into conflict with our personal agenda. At that point, what is good becomes what *we've* decided is good. What is fair becomes what *we've* decided is fair.

In reality, though, God alone is the arbiter of fairness. Israel was God's chosen people, and as such was given the Promised Land. Why Israel? Were they better or less rebellious than the other nations? Even a cursory reading of the Old Testament will quickly dispel that notion. Why Israel? Because God is God, and God decided to choose Israel. "Jacob I loved and Esau I hated" (Rom 9:13). Why Jacob? Wasn't he a deceiver, a manipulator, a conniver? A review of Jacob's character traits and exploits might leave you unimpressed. In fact, if you were deciding which brother to hang out with, you'd probably choose Esau. Why Jacob? Because God is God, and God decided to bless Jacob.

The list goes on. Only Aaron's line was allowed to be priests. David was forgiven his horrific sins of adultery and murder, but Achan's entire family was destroyed because of his sin of covetousness. Gideon asked for a sign from God and received two; Zechariah asked for a sign from God and was struck dumb for his unbelief. Jonah preached God's judgment and Nineveh repented; Jeremiah preached God's judgment and Judah persecuted and imprisoned him. Go figure.

I'm not sure where we got the idea that, with regard to wealth transfer, fairness demands equality, but I can assure you it didn't come from God's word. On the contrary, what was commanded and modeled with regard to the land inheritance is actually quite the opposite. Not only was inequality permitted by God, at times it was commanded. Allow me to share several examples.

The Double-Portion

Those familiar with the Old Testament might remember that one sibling was required by God to receive a larger inheritance than the others.

> *If a man has two wives, and he loves one but not the other, and both bear him sons but the firstborn is the son of the wife he does not love, when he wills his property to his sons, he must not give **the rights of the firstborn** to the son of the wife he loves in preference to his actual firstborn, the son of the wife he does not love. **He must acknowledge the son of his unloved wife as the firstborn by giving him a double share of all he has. That son is the first sign of his father's strength. The right of the firstborn belongs to him.*** (Deuteronomy 21:15-17, emphasis mine)

It was the God-ordained practice of Jewish families to honor the rights of the firstborn son by giving him double the amount of inheritance that would be received by his siblings. My point here is not to argue in favor of this particular practice for our day and time, but rather to point out one of several inheritance practices God gave to Israel that was inherently unequal.

Size of family

This principle seemed so obvious and common sense when I read it that I was surprised it hadn't occurred to me before. When the time came for Israel's leaders to divide the Promised Land among the various tribes and families, God instructed Moses to take the family size into consideration in allocating the land.

> The Lord said to Moses, "The land is to be allotted to them as an inheritance based on the number of names. **To a larger group give a larger inheritance, and to a smaller group a smaller one**; each is to receive its inheritance according to the number of those listed." (Numbers 26:52-54, emphasis mine)

This is brilliant! Imagine making an inheritance decision based on the size of the family receiving it. Seems obvious, doesn't it? It stands to reason that an adult child who decides to remain unmarried or childless will have an entirely different financial need than the adult child with six biological kids and two adopted special needs children. The main point, though, is that God felt no obligation to equalize the land distribution. Rather than give every adult child's family an equal share, each family received their allotment based on the size of their family, i.e. their need. Interestingly, there is no biblical account of recipient families complaining to God that His decision to distribute the Promised Land based on family size was "unfair."

Sons or daughters

Do you remember which particular heirs were allowed to inherit a family's land, and which were prohibited from doing so? Strange as it may seem to our equality-oriented sensibilities, God had determined that only sons were allowed to inherit the land.

> *After the plague the Lord said to Moses and Eleazar son of Aaron, the priest, "Take a census of the whole Israelite community by families—all those twenty years old or more who are able to serve in the army of Israel." So on the plains of Moab by the Jordan across from Jericho, Moses and Eleazar the priest spoke with them and said, "**Take a census of the men twenty years old or more**, as the Lord commanded Moses..."*
>
> *The **total number of the men of Israel** was 601,730. The Lord said to Moses, "**The land is to be allotted to them** as an inheritance based on the number of names."* (Numbers 26:1-4, 51-53, emphasis mine)

When the land was being divided and allotment instructions given, it was made clear that daughters were not included, either in the initial allotment of land or through subsequent inheritance. Why would God instruct Israel to pass the inheritance down to sons, but not daughters? Most likely because it was expected that the daughters would marry, and as such would enjoy the benefits of the land owned by their husbands. The sons are the ones who had the responsibility to care for their new families once married, and the land inheritance was an important part of this responsibility.

In at least one case, however, this prohibition against daughters receiving a land inheritance raised a particular concern, one important enough for Moses to consider making an exception.

The daughters of Zelophehad son of Hepher, the son of Gilead, the son of Makir, the son of Manasseh, belonged to the clans of Manasseh son of Joseph. The names of the daughters were Mahlah, Noah, Hoglah, Milkah and Tirzah. They came forward and stood before Moses, Eleazar the priest, the leaders and the whole assembly at the entrance to the tent of meeting and said, "Our father died in the wilderness. He was not among Korah's followers, who banded together against the Lord, but he died for his own sin and left no sons. **Why should our father's name disappear from his clan because he had no son?** *Give* *us property among our father's relatives."* (Numbers 27:1-4, emphasis mine)

Moses consulted the Lord and was instructed to honor this request, albeit with certain restrictions. As noted above, my point is not to argue for our repeating this Old Covenant practice that was unique to Israel and served a particular set of God's purposes with the land He'd entrusted to them. Rather, my objective is to demonstrate that this first principle of wealth transfer is decidedly biblical and talk about ways we might apply this principle to inheritance in 21st century America.

Application

All of us, who have been saved by God's grace through faith in Jesus Christ, will agree with the oft-stated reality that, "the ground is level at the foot of the cross." God does not show favoritism. This is the sense in which our desire for fairness and equality is truly a reflection of God's image in us. We've come to despise every form of prejudice, oppression and deprivation of human rights. This is admirable. But we must let go of our unbiblical assumption that equality demands equal distribution of resources. Or that inequality with regard to inheritance is inherently unfair. In God's economy, inequality was not only permitted, but was in some instances required.

How then can we apply this first principle to our wealth transfer plans? Following are several examples of situations that might lead Christian parents to seriously consider unequal estate distribution.

1. **Varying income levels:** Some of our adult children may have done very well financially, while some might be struggling just to make ends meet. The surgeon earning $800K/year has a different financial need than the executive earning $150K and the teacher making $45K/year.

2. **Size of families:** The adult child with eight children has an entirely different level of financial responsibility than the one with two children. Different still is the need of the adult child who has decided not to have children at all.

3. **Financial needs within families:** Individual financial needs that should be considered include: an adult child whose spouse is deceased (especially if that spouse was the primary wage-earner); those who have one or more special needs children or children with expensive medical needs; those whose children have particular educational needs or opportunities.

4. **Family business:** In many instances, not all of the adult children have chosen to work in the family business. This is a case where equal distribution, i.e. dividing ownership of the business equally between all the kids, can result in irreparable damage, not only to the business but also to the sibling relationships.

So, the first step in considering how to divide the portion of your estate that will pass to your children is to evaluate, not only financial need, but also various other factors that might result in unequal distribution decisions. Going through this process doesn't necessarily mean you'll choose unequal distribution, but it might well lead in that direction.

I should point out that the next three biblical inheritance principles will also have a bearing on your decisions with regard to equal vs. unequal distribution. Let's go on to the second principle.

Principle 1. Inequality is Permitted

CHAPTER 11

REQUESTS ARE ACCEPTABLE

I t is not uncommon for a parent to bristle when an adult child initiates discussion about their desire to inherit a particular estate asset. Such requests are usually not considered a problem if they are limited to personal property, the value of which is primarily sentimental: a family heirloom, a piece of mom's jewelry or the china that has been passed down from prior generations. Requests related to such items are often welcomed. The parents' response changes quickly, though, when the request involves higher-priced and more substantial estate assets, such as the vacation property, family business or a stated preference for liquid vs. illiquid assets. Such requests are often met with frustration, even anger that the kids are 'already planning for our death so they can get their hands on their inheritance.' But are such requests unreasonable?

Christian parents with wealth often deceive themselves into believing the kids a) "have no idea how much we have" and b) "don't really have an expectation" with regard to inheritance. This inaccurate belief is what leads to frustration when one of the kids broaches the subject. I've spent a considerable amount of time with the next generation and I can tell you unequivocally: they have an idea and they have an expectation. Granted, your adult kids' idea of how much wealth you have might not be accurate, but they most certainly have an idea. This is why we parents should be willing to engage our adult kids in this discussion, and why we shouldn't get frustrated when they bring it up.

How should we deal with the issue of inheritance requests? Let's first look at a couple examples from Scripture where such requests were made.

Transjordan Tribes' Request

This is one of the more amusing misunderstandings you'll find in the Bible, though I'm sure it wasn't seen as funny at the time. As Israel was working her way toward the Promised Land at the end of Moses' life, the Reubenites and Gadites recognized how ideal the land east of the Jordan River would be to accommodate their vast flocks and herds. They reasoned that, rather than receiving their land inheritance west of the Jordan along with the other tribes, it would be better to request land they deemed much more suitable for their live-stock and way of life. They approached Moses to discuss this request.

Due to an initial misunderstanding, Moses' first response (*"Shall your countrymen go to war while you sit here?"*) was less than favorable. Once these tribes clarified their intentions, however, Moses softened his stance.

> *Then they came up to him and said, "We would like to build pens here for our livestock and cities for our women and children. But we will arm ourselves for battle and go ahead of the Israelites until we have brought them to their place. Meanwhile our women and children will live in fortified cities, for protection from the inhabitants of the land. We will not return to our homes until each of the Israelites has received their inheritance. We will not receive any inheritance with them on the other side of the Jordan, because our inheritance has come to us on the east side of the Jordan."* (Numbers 32:16-19)

Once the concern was eliminated as to these tribes' commitment to Israel and her mission, Moses immediately granted their request on the condition they honor their pledge to go into battle with their fellow Israelites and help them to secure the Promised Land.

> *Then Moses gave to the Gadites, the Reubenites and the half-tribe of Manasseh son of Joseph the kingdom of Sihon king of the Amorites and the kingdom of Og*

*king of Bashan—the whole land with its cities and the
territory around them.* (Numbers 32:33)

This is one example of a specific inheritance request being made
that God (through Moses) agreed to grant. Mind you, honoring this
request was not automatic. As was the case with the daughters of
Zelophehad discussed in the last chapter, this request was condition-
ally granted. The agreement would have been forfeit had they proven
unfaithful, i.e. failed to honor their part of the commitment. Even
so, a reasonable request was made and the conditions surrounding
approval were honored, so the Transjordan tribes received their
inheritance as requested.

Another example of a specific land request came from Caleb.

Caleb's Request

For many of us, Joshua and Caleb stand as pillars of the faith,
godly Old Testament heroes after whom we name our sons and seek
to pattern our lives. When Moses sent twelve spies to explore the
Promised Land, ten of the twelve returned with a troubling perspective. Unbelieving, unfaithful and completely ignoring God's promises, the negative report they gave brought a sense of fear and dread
on the Israelites. Not so with Joshua and Caleb, whose good report
overflowed with confidence in the God who had promised the land
and who would fight for Israel as they entered to take possession of

it. Israel's failure to listen to Joshua and Caleb resulted in forty years of wandering in the desert before Israel would have a second opportunity to receive their promised inheritance.

Fast-forward four-plus decades. The Promised Land has for the most part been conquered and the land is being divided among the tribes and families of Israel. Caleb has his eye on a particular piece of land he had observed when he first entered the land as a spy more than forty years earlier. Since Moses had promised Caleb a piece of the *"land he set his feet on, because he followed the Lord whole-heartedly"* (Dt 1:36), Caleb approached Joshua to make his request.

> *"Now then, just as the Lord promised, he has kept me alive for forty-five years since the time he said this to Moses, while Israel moved about in the wilderness. So here I am today, eighty-five years old! I am still as strong today as the day Moses sent me out; I'm just as vigorous to go out to battle now as I was then.* **Now give me this hill country that the Lord promised me that day.** *You yourself heard then that the Anakites were there and their cities were large and fortified, but, the Lord helping me, I will drive them out just as he said." Then Joshua blessed Caleb son of Jephunneh and gave him Hebron as his inheritance.* (Joshua 14:10:13, emphasis mine)

Caleb's request was granted without conditions because he'd already proven himself faithful.

Joshua's Request

As Joshua and the other leaders were concluding the process of dividing the land, the last allotment mentioned was that requested by Joshua himself.

> *When they had finished dividing the land into its allotted portions, the Israelites gave Joshua son of Nun an inheritance among them, as the Lord had commanded. **They gave him the town he asked for—** Timnath Serah in the hill country of Ephraim. And he built up the town and settled there.* (Joshua 19:49-50, emphasis mine)

As was true of the Transjordan Tribes and Caleb, Joshua asked for a particular part of the inheritance and it was granted to him.

Application

In all three of the above examples, specific inheritance requests by the heirs were entertained without rebuke. (Moses' initial rebuke of the Transjordan Tribes was not due to their making the request, but because he thought they were abandoning the mission.) How should we apply this principle to our estate planning process? The first step is to invite or initiate this discussion with your adult kids, especially if you own any of the types of assets that could trigger problems for your heirs. A few specific examples come immediately to mind:

1. **Family business:** As noted in the prior chapter, there are many cases in which not all of the adult children are working in the family business. When this is the case, it might be more desirable – it's certainly more practical – to allow the business to be inherited only by the adult child or children who are working there. Otherwise there is likely to be an ongoing conflict among the siblings with regard to the disposition of profits, i.e. the extent to which they are reinvested for future growth vs. distributed as dividends.

2. **Family home, vacation home, building lots:** It is not unusual for a vacation home enjoyed by the entire family while the kids were growing up to be used by only one or two of the adults kids once they all have families of their own. This is a case where it is reasonable to discuss the adult kids' preferences with regard to inheriting this property. Those using the vacation home will likely be much more willing to keep it (and pay for annual maintenance, insurance and property taxes) than their siblings who have no intention of using the property. The same may be true for your other real estate.

73

3. **Furniture, jewelry, collectibles, boat or motorcycle:** This is self-explanatory but certainly worth mentioning. In many cases, dividing (or liquidating) the personal property is handled with relative ease because none of the adult kids have a personal attachment. But what happens when they do? One of your daughters might cherish several pieces of mom's jewelry, either because she likes jewelry or for sentimental reasons. Her sister who doesn't wear jewelry would rather have the cash the estate would generate by selling it all. Same for art collections, large or small, some of your furniture (especially antiques) or the family boat. Best to sort these preferences out while you're alive than to leave the kids to fight it out once you're gone. Some of these pieces of property might best be given before your death, just so there is no question as to your preferred distribution.

4. **Liquid vs. illiquid assets:** This can be a major issue when an estate is divided equally between the kids. Your adult kids who are in good shape financially can afford, and might not mind, owning illiquid assets. Others, those for whom finances have been more of a struggle, have no interest in, and might not benefit from, inheriting illiquid assets, especially if they are non-income producing (e.g. raw land, building lots, an art or car collection). If a portion of your estate is illiquid, it might be wise to work through this issue ahead of time so you can try to accommodate reasonable requests made by

your heirs. You might even decide to liquidate some of these assets during your lifetime to simplify the estate administration process for the kids.

Have you ever had one of your adult children approach you to discuss a specific request with regard to your estate? If so, how did you respond? If not, how might you respond? Given the fact that biblical wisdom suggests it is okay for the kids to initiate this discussion, I would propose it is equally prudent for the parents to invite them to do so. After all, many of our kids, who have strong inheritance preferences, might hesitate to bring their requests to mom and dad because they are concerned about how this discussion might be received. One of the significant benefits of Christian parents encouraging this particular discussion is that it potentially avoids hurt feelings, resentment and sibling squabbling down the road.

Let's turn our attention now to a somewhat more complex issue: setting inheritance limits.

Principle 1. Inequality is Permitted
Principle 2. Requests are Acceptable

CHAPTER 12

LIMITATIONS ARE PRUDENT

If you've ever spent time studying biblical financial principles or read a book on the subject, one of the first concepts you encountered was the clear teaching that God owns everything. I shared some sample verses in an earlier chapter that affirm God's ownership of all resources, and we can add to those passages God's stated ownership of us as well (Rom 14:8, for example). Even the ability we have to accumulate financial resources comes directly from God (Deut 8:18). It all belongs to Him, and for the most part, God's people readily acknowledge this truth.

For that reason, it has always intrigued me as to why so few Christians with excess wealth leave any part of it to Kingdom work, and why the relatively small percentage of those who do typically leave far more of God's wealth to their adult children than to His work, regardless of the size of their estate. We might give intellectual and verbal assent to the concept of God's ownership, but when it comes to planning for the disposition of our estates, our actions betray us. For many of us, our estate planning documents convey the belief that the money and property does, in fact, belong to us, and as such we are free from Divine input as to the distribution of these assets.

It could well be that we are willfully ignoring God's ownership in the wealth transfer process, but I'm convinced that many or most of us simply haven't given it much thought. For the most part, we might not even have given any input into our estate documents; we hired an estate attorney, gave them a list of our assets and the names of our kids, and off they went. We signed the documents put before us by the professional we hired, then stuck the documents in a desk drawer or safe until it was time for the next estate plan review. Our current estate plan might have one hundred percent of the assets transferring to the kids equally, but this decision was probably made by default, not as a result of thoughtful planning or an attempt to apply God's inheritance principles.

So how might biblical wisdom instruct us differently? Let's consider the specific limitations God chose to place on the inheritance given to His people.

Limitations for Israel

If you look at a map of the Middle East and then identify the piece of land given by God to the twelve tribes of Israel, something should immediately jump out at you: it's really not very big. Expand to a map of Europe and Asia, and the Promised Land is barely noticeable. A map of the Eastern Hemisphere obscures it completely. Even if we eliminate from consideration the land that had not yet been discovered or inhabited during O.T. times, Israel's inheritance – from a size perspective, anyway – barely registered on the world map.

None of us who've read through the Bible would ever question God's immense love for His beloved nation of Israel. Why then, did God choose to place such severe limitations on the amount of land His children would inherit? We've already discussed the fact that *The earth is the Lord's, and everything in it, the world, and all who live in it* (Psalm 24:1). Given the fact that God, then as now, owned all of the land in the world, it is interesting that He decided to pass down only a relatively small portion of what He owned as Israel's inheritance.

> *"I will establish your borders from the Red Sea to the Mediterranean Sea, and from the desert to the Euphrates River."* (Exodus 23:31)

God chose to establish clearly defined borders, or limitations, on Israel's inheritance despite His ownership of all land in existence. This same practice was applied as the land was being divided among the tribes and families.

Limitations for Tribes

Chapters 13 through 19 of the book of Joshua provide elaborate detail of the division of the land among the tribes of Israel. For example:

The allotment for Joseph began at the Jordan, east
of the springs of Jericho, and went up from there
through the desert into the hill country of Bethel. It
went on from Bethel (that is, Luz), crossed over to the
territory of the Arkites in Ataroth, descended west-
ward to the territory of the Japhletites as far as the
region of Lower Beth Horon and on to Gezer, ending
at the Mediterranean Sea. (Joshua 16:1-3)

Each tribe of Israel received a limited, clearly defined piece of the land. The same was true of the allocation along family lines.

Limitations for Families

As described in the chapter on inequality, further division of the Promised Land along family lines was to take into consideration family size. This is not only an example of unequal distribution, but also of limitations being placed on the amount inherited.

The Lord said to Moses, "The land is to be allotted to
them as an inheritance based on the number of names.
To a larger group give a larger inheritance, and to a
smaller group a smaller one; each is to receive its
inheritance according to the number of those listed.
Be sure that the land is distributed by lot. What each

79

group inherits will be according to the names for its
ancestral tribe. Each inheritance is to be distrib-
uted by lot among the larger and smaller groups."
(Numbers 26:52-56)

As has been the case throughout, I'm not suggesting this passage creates a mandate to design your inheritance limitations around
family size (or for that matter by casting lots). You may decide to take
family size into consideration, but it is only one of many variables
that should be part of your thought process. The point is that in all
three cases, nation, tribe and family, there were limitations placed
on the amount that would be inherited, and the total amount inherited reflected only a relatively small portion of what the Father had
available to pass down.

Application

I can't help wondering how the 21st century American church
would have responded had we been the group of God's people
receiving the Promised Land. How might we have reacted to these
'extreme' limitations being placed on our inheritance? We might have
wondered why, with all the land in the world at His disposal, God
decided to leave us so little. And why did He pick this particular piece
of land? Hawaii was empty at the time. Wouldn't that have been a
better choice? I can hear us now: "It's not fair!"

But I digress. Let's consider several examples of cases in which we might seriously consider placing limitations on the amount passed down to our adult children.

1. **Compromising Their Work Ethic:** An inheritance amount that ensures our adult children will not have to work in order to provide for their families might not be a good idea. Diligent work is God's primary means of enabling us to care for our families' needs. Providing some degree of financial assistance through inheritance can be a great blessing, but leaving so much wealth to our kids that neither spouse has to work any longer is neither honoring to God or in our kids' best interest. (Exceptions might include making it possible for one spouse to stay home with the kids, or assisting with a transition to the ministry, non-profit or volunteer work they feel God is calling them to. Be careful in the latter case, though. Many are the young adults who, given access to a large inheritance or trust fund, suddenly decide they are sensing God's call to ministry, a 'calling' that was never mentioned or considered before the money became available. In many cases, they just don't like their present job, boss, regular hours or accountability.)

2. **Emasculating Our Sons-in-Law:** If you have married daughters, please listen carefully. One of the most damaging things we can do as parents is to rob our sons-in-law of their

81

ability – and responsibility – to provide for our daughters. Leaving our daughters independently wealthy not only steals their husband's dignity, but also threatens his role in the marriage. What happens when there is a disagreement about a major spending decision? When our daughters want something their family income can't afford – and/or their husbands disagree with purchasing – what is the impact on marital unity when mom and dad have provided a blank check? Note that this problem can exist both after death (via inheritance) and during lifetime (via interference). Please don't do this to your sons-in-law.

3. **Lack of Maturity:** We need to be very cautious about passing down a significant amount of wealth to adult children who have never demonstrated the maturity to handle it well. Maturity is not always an age issue. Some of our adult children continue to demonstrate immaturity in their financial decision-making well into adulthood. Examples of financial immaturity might include a history of: gullibility, such as falling for get-rich-quick schemes; making large purchases on credit with no understanding of the repayment terms; continually giving or loaning money to free-loading friends or relatives while failing to discern a pattern of abuse. Restricting the age at which the inheritance is available might help, but only if the immature adult child suddenly matures before that particular age. My guess is that kids struggling

with financial maturity when they don't have a lot of money are not likely to suddenly mature when a lot of money is dropped on them.

4. **Encouraging Materialism and Excessive Lifestyles:** We know our kids, and for those who are married, we also know their spouses. Are we observing a tendency toward poor spending decisions or lifestyle choices? Some of our adult kids have only been protected from a highly consumptive, debt-ridden lifestyle by their limited resources and a restricted amount of available credit. Are they frequently verbalizing all the major purchases they would make if they just had more money? Do they consistently communicate dissatisfaction with their standard of living and a lack of contentment in general? If the size of their pending inheritance is likely to trigger or fuel this unhealthy focus on material possessions, we need to seriously consider limitations.

In closing this chapter, I'd like to take a step back from the individual child/family inheritance amount and consider the total estate. God's allocation to Israel, as we discussed, was only a portion of the wealth He owned. As I mentioned earlier, only a small percentage of Christians leave any money to God's work in their wills, and those who do typically limit charitable giving to a relatively small portion of their estate. Why is this? I think the problem is that we use the wrong starting point in our estate planning process.

The default starting point is that 100% of our estates will be divided between the kids equally. Most of us stop there. Those inclined to give a portion to God's work move on to the second question: How much should we leave to the Kingdom? I would like to humbly suggest that we have it backwards. One hundred percent of our estate belongs to God. We'll only die with the portion we didn't consume or give away during our lifetime, i.e. the excess. Since all of this money belongs to God and all of it represents money entrusted to us that we were never going to need or use, shouldn't our default assumption be that *most or all* of the excess was intended for His work? Rather than asking ourselves how much we can justify giving to charity, shouldn't we rather ask ourselves how much we can justify giving to our adult kids, all of whom have the exact same responsibility to provide for their own families that we had for ours?

Here's my suggestion for all Christians with excess wealth that will be available as an inheritance. Instead of adhering to the default assumption that everything should go to the kids and we just have to decide whether or how much to give to God's work, let's commit to taking the opposite approach. Let's begin by assuming that 100% of the excess money God entrusted to us is supposed to be left to God's work. Then we can, in view of our eventual opportunity to stand before Jesus and give an account for what we did with His money (Matthew 25:14-30), begin to consider how much of His money He would have us pass along to our kids.

This approach will not only change the wealth transfer discussion, but it will almost certainly change the results. We earlier acknowledged that *a good person leaves an inheritance for their children's children* (Proverbs 13:22). Leaving an inheritance is one thing; leaving our heirs independently wealthy so they don't have to work, make wise financial decisions or learn to rely on God is a curse, not a blessing. Let's not dishonor God in this way and let's not use His resources to harm the next generation. Limitations on the amount to be passed down are very, very prudent.

To summarize, the starting point for the wealth transfer discussion should be the assumption that God gets it all because God owns it all. Only then can we begin to prudently and prayerfully assess which portion of our estate God would delight to see us pass to our heirs. This approach, incidentally, is the cure for Inheritolatry.

Principle 1. Inequality is Permitted

Principle 2. Requests are Acceptable

Principle 3. Limitations are Prudent

CHAPTER 13

RESPONSIBILITY IS REQUIRED

F ew topics are more painful for Christian parents to discuss than adult children who have rejected the faith. Only slightly less painful is watching our adult kids who are professing Christians live irresponsibly, having drifted away from church and demonstrating little or no interest in God's word, spiritual disciplines or Christian fellowship. Unfortunately, this reality is epidemic in our current culture.

From a purely secular perspective, the thought of reducing or even eliminating (gasp!) an adult child's inheritance because they rejected God or have been consistently irresponsible with regard to money sounds harsh at best, fanatical at worst. But what about God's perspective? How should we approach the wealth transfer decision with regard to an adult child who fails to honor God as God, who loves the things of this world or who has a history making unbiblical financial decisions? As we'll see, God takes this issue very seriously.

There are several types of irresponsibility noted in the Scriptures, and the Lord doesn't seem to be particularly fond of any of them.

Regardless of the type of unfaithfulness being demonstrated, God's solution is very consistent. How strongly does God feel about tying inheritance to responsibility? Consider the following examples.

Ignoring God's Authority

Once the conquest of Canaan was substantially complete and the land was being divided among the tribes, clans and families, Joshua issued the following warning to Israel concerning her land inheritance:

> *"But just as all the good things the Lord your God has promised you have come to you, so he will bring on you all the evil things he has threatened, until the Lord your God has destroyed you from this good land he has given you.* ***If you violate the covenant of the Lord your God, which he commanded you, and go and serve other gods and bow down to them, the Lord's anger will burn against you, and you will quickly perish from the good land he has given you."***
> (Joshua 23:15-16, emphasis mine)

As much as God loved Israel and as gracious as he'd been in providing this land as her inheritance, God made clear that if she were to *"turn away"* (v. 12), violating His covenant and serving other gods,

Israel would lose her inheritance and be removed from the land. Note the particularly strong language used in this warning.

Another interesting passage to consider is in Ezra chapter ten. Ezra was leading God's people in corporate confession and repentance for their blatant disregard for God's authority. This gathering was immediately followed by a proclamation for all Israel:

> *A proclamation was then issued throughout Judah and Jerusalem for all the exiles to assemble in Jerusalem. Anyone who failed to appear within three days* **would forfeit all his property**, *in accordance with the decision of the officials and elders, and would himself be expelled from the assembly of the exiles.* (Ezra 10:7-8, emphasis mine)

I found it interesting that the penalty for failing to honor God's authority as exercised through His leaders, even in something as basic as attending the assembly of His people, included forfeiture of all property. As noted above, this is an issue God seems to take very seriously.

Disobedience, Sin and Idolatry

In the following passage, God is giving Moses explicit instructions concerning sinful behavior that will not be tolerated among His people. After listing a number of particular sins from which Israel must abstain, He warns:

> *"Do not defile yourselves in any of these ways, because this is how the nations that I am going to drive out before you became defiled. Even the land was defiled; so I punished it for its sin, and the land vomited out its inhabitants. But you must keep my decrees and my laws. The native-born and the foreigners residing among you must not do any of these detestable things, for all these things were done by the people who lived in the land before you, and the land became defiled. **And if you defile the land, it will vomit you out as it vomited out the nations that were before you**.* (Leviticus 18:24-28, emphasis mine)

We find this caution repeated in the book of Jeremiah, the prophet through whom God issued a similar warning:

> *My mountain in the land and **your wealth and all your treasures I will give away as plunder**, together with your high places, because of sin throughout your country. **Through your own fault you will lose the inheritance I gave you**. I will enslave you to your enemies in a land you do not know, for you have kindled*

89

my anger, and it will burn forever." (Jeremiah 17:1-4, emphasis mine)

This is another instance in which irresponsible behavior results in the loss of an inheritance that would otherwise have been retained. Granted, ignoring God's authority and willfully disobeying His commands are among the more extreme versions of irresponsibility. Can He possibly feel as strongly about someone who simply mismanages money?

Unfaithful Stewardship

Jesus continued this theme when teaching on financial responsibility in two parables: The Parable of the Talents in Matthew 25 and The Parable of the Ten Minas in Luke 19. For those unfamiliar with these parables, observe the owner's response to the servant who failed to manage well the resources entrusted to him:

> *His master replied, 'You wicked, lazy servant! So you knew that I harvest where I have not sown and gather where I have not scattered seed? Well then, you should have put my money on deposit with the bankers, so that when I returned I would have received it back with interest.' So **take the bag of gold from him and give it to the one who has ten bags**. For whoever has*

will be given more, and they will have an abundance. Whoever does not have, even what they have will be taken from them. (Matthew 25:26-29)

*His master replied, 'I will judge you by your own words, you wicked servant! You knew, did you, that I am a hard man, taking out what I did not put in, and reaping what I did not sow? Why then didn't you put my money on deposit, so that when I came back, I could have collected it with interest?' Then he said to those standing by, '**Take his mina away from him and give it to the one who has ten minas**.''* (Luke 19:24-25)

Although these parables are very similar and sometimes mistaken to be parallel passages, the contrasts (e.g. number of servants, amount, distribution) make clear that these are two different parables taught on two separate occasions. What is the primary emphasis of both passages? First, those who prove unfaithful in their management of God's resources will not only fail to receive additional resources, but even what has originally been entrusted to them will be taken away. Second, those who do prove faithful as stewards will be given more to manage.

It may be challenging to apply this 'faithfulness screen' to our wealth transfer plans, but I believe God's ownership requires that we take this issue as seriously as He does. Otherwise *we* become the unfaithful stewards and risk having the resources He's entrusted to us taken away. Remember, they were God's resources before we received them, they are His while we are managing them, and they'll continue to be His after we've passed them on. In God's economy, faithful stewardship is non-negotiable.

Application

This list of "responsibility" passages is not exhaustive, but I hope it is instructive. There is no easy way to say this: those who have proven themselves irresponsible before God – whether through resisting His authority, living in sinful disobedience, or simply poor and unbiblical financial management – will forfeit those resources that would otherwise be entrusted to them. There may be, and often are, other temporal consequences for disobedience and irresponsibility, but in all cases listed above, one immediate result was the forfeiture of financial resources, both current resources and those to be inherited.

Unlike our salvation, which is unconditionally given to those who repent and trust in Jesus (Rom 6:23; Rom 10:9) and can never be forfeit (John 10:28; Rom 8:38-39), when God entrusts financial resources to His people, the blessing is often conditional. We are accountable to God for the way we manage both our lives and His resources. Responsibility is required. It will be difficult for us to give an account to the Owner if we've disregarded His teaching on this important topic. This is, perhaps, the most difficult issue we'll have to consider in designing our wealth transfer plans, but it would be unwise to ignore it.

What are some examples of cases in which passing God's wealth to an adult child would represent poor stewardship of his resources and might even prove damaging to the recipient?

1. **Pursuing a sinful lifestyle:** It is not possible to objectively read the Bible and conclude that it is wise to allocate a significant portion of God's wealth to an adult child who is living in willful violation of God's instructions. At the very least such an inheritance should be limited and have thoughtful restrictions placed on it, but serious consideration must also be given to forfeiture. This is especially true in cases where there have been problems with addiction, or destructive behavior of any kind.

2. **Persistent financial irresponsibility:** God's word is clear that those who are unwise and unfaithful in the management of His material resources will not be given more to manage. On the contrary, what little they have already been given may well be taken away from them. Do you have adult children who on more than one occasion have needed you to bail them out of financial difficulty? Or kids who never seem to learn from their financial mistakes? When we've observed over the

93

years a persistent pattern of making poor financial decisions – whether spending, borrowing or investment decisions – we need to think twice about adding fuel to the fire.

3. **Refuses stewardship instruction:** Often times, financial irresponsibility is the result of a lack of education and training rather than blatant disregard for God and His word. The best way to distinguish between the two root causes is to offer stewardship instruction. There are plenty of good books, sermons and Bible studies on this topic that we can make available to our adult kids, and some Christian parents will offer to pay for biblically based financial planning for their adult kids as part of their stewardship training. (This is a particularly good idea for Christian parents who expect to leave an inheritance.) Offering such instruction will help you quickly discern whether the adult child's pattern of irresponsibility is due to lack of education or willful disobedience. If the latter is true, they'll have no interest in the training or resources you've suggested.

4. **Adult child is a "lover of money":** King Solomon made a profound statement in Ecclesiastes 5:10. *Whoever loves money never has enough; whoever loves wealth is never satisfied with their income.* We've seen this on a daily basis in our materialistic culture and some of us have personally struggled in this area over the years. Sadly, many of our adult children, having grown up experiencing both the blessings

and trappings of wealth, have allowed money to become their god. Like the rich fool in Jesus' parable (Luke 12:13-21), there is an endless pursuit of wealth, often accompanied by a sense of material entitlement. Those who serve money cannot serve God (Luke 16:13), and giving more of God's wealth to those already serving money will only push them further away from Him.

Note that the decision to limit or eliminate an heir's inheritance, as in the above cases, doesn't always have to be permanent or irreversible. There are ways to structure our testamentary trusts so this action can be reversed should the adult child change course and begin to walk faithfully before the Lord. An experienced estate attorney, who shares your biblical worldview, can help with this process.

Remember that we're dealing with God's wealth, not ours. As such, being found faithful by the Owner should be of far greater concern to us than the possibility of disappointing our kids. Surely we should continue to love them, pray for them, encourage them and be a witness to them – both living and verbal. We never stop pleading with God to draw our wandering kids to Himself, and we never stop exhorting our kids to turn to Him. The issue isn't whether or not we continue to love and pray for them, but whether is it prudent and biblical to leave a significant amount of God's wealth to an adult child who will not acknowledge either His ownership or their accountability, and who are therefore highly unlikely to use inherited wealth for God's glory.

To summarize, here are the four biblical inheritance principles that need to be considered in our estate planning and wealth transfer process:

Principle 1. Inequality is Permitted

Principle 2. Requests are Acceptable

Principle 3. Limitations are Prudent

Principle 4. Responsibility is Required

CHAPTER 14

THE RESULTS

P rior to coming to faith in Jesus Christ, I struggled mightily with greed, covetousness and materialism. Once I gave my life to the Lord at age thirty-two and began studying His word, I found myself immediately conflicted. Most of what I'd learned and believed as a secular financial advisor was diametrically opposed to what I was reading in God's word. I thought my income and assets belonged to me; God said they are His. I believed the aggressive pursuit of money and material possessions signaled success; God said it signaled idolatry. I'd been taught that debt provided freedom because it allowed me to buy things I could not yet afford; God said debt creates bondage. I was certain that I was accountable only to myself for my financial decisions; God said I am accountable to Him.

It got worse. I thought radical generosity meant throwing a $10 bill into the collection basket instead of a couple $1's or the change in my pocket; God said obedience begins with giving ten percent of my income and that I should cheerfully increase giving as He prospers me. It was at this point – giving generously to God's work – I initially rebelled. Or at least tried to rebel.

I still remember the day a pastor friend was explaining to me what God's word had to say about giving and generosity. He must have been amused by my response when I asked what the Bible meant by giving a "tithe." I wasn't impressed with his answer. "Ten percent? Of my entire income? You've got to be crazy!"

I didn't know what God's word said about money at that point, but I was pretty sure it didn't say that. So I searched the Scriptures, focusing particularly on the issue of giving and generosity. Sure enough, and at first very much to my chagrin, my pastor friend was right. Despite my heart's natural resistance, I kept reading, asking God to help me understand His truth. Then an amazing thing happened. My initial rebellion quickly melted away under the tutelage of God the Holy Spirit, and my heart began to soften. Not only did I find myself submitting to God's instruction on giving – I actually began to embrace it with joy and gratitude. I can honestly say that no financial decision I've made since that time has come close to the blessing of giving generously.

Implementation Challenges

The reason I shared this bit of personal history is because I understand the initial tension and stress many readers experienced as you worked through the four biblical inheritance principles. At some point in each chapter your thoughts might have drifted from the theological to the practical, from reviewing the Bible passages to make sure I've correctly interpreted them to, "How in the world am I going to explain this to my kids?" Typical first responses to this information will range from disbelief to confusion to outright rebellion as the implications hit home. For that reason, some will put this book away and try to quickly forget its contents. It's much easier to leave things as they are than to deal with the painful complexity of revising your estate plan to bring it into conformity with these four principles.

If this describes you, I would ask that you do one thing before adding this book to your stack of those to be donated to the used-Christian-books store. Go back and review the Scriptures in the previous four chapters. Ignore my words completely if you like, but don't ignore God's. If you determine that I've incorrectly understood and conveyed God's word, you can and should disregard what I've said. If, however, God's words have been accurately represented and applied, please don't make the mistake of ignoring His instructions simply because they are difficult to implement.

Understanding Our Objections

I had thought about including a Q&A section at this point in the text to identify and address the most common objections that often arise when having this inheritance discussion. The problem I ran into with this approach, however, is that in one way or another, the answer to every objection is the same: it's God's money, not ours. In teaching and counseling on this subject, I've learned that most objections have nothing to do with disagreement about each principle's biblical underpinning; the objections are based on the challenges we anticipate with implementation.

For example, I might have been quickly persuaded that God put strict limitations on Israel's inheritance and only passed down a small portion of what He had available. God's word is pretty clear on this issue. But when I think about actually having to explain to the kids my decision to limit their inheritance to a relatively small portion of my total estate so I can maximize the amount available for Kingdom work, tension and anxiety immediately ensues. I might write-off the idea of limiting inheritance, not because I don't believe it is biblical, but because I don't want to deal with the implementation challenges and potential relational fallout.

What is interesting is that our adult kids, whose spiritual commitment and maturity are such that they *should* receive an inheritance, will be the first to insist we leave the money to God's work rather than to them. It is typically our less responsible, uncommitted and straying adult kids who will most strenuously object to this approach to estate planning. I can't help but think that when our adult kids raise a strong objection to our application of these principles, they are simply affirming our wisdom in limiting their inheritance amount. An adult child's anger over not receiving as much as he or she feels entitled to is proof positive that placing the limitation was the wise thing to do.

Just as the visceral objection to the biblical concept of sin by our unsaved friends simply confirms their separation from God, the angry objection to the biblical concept of limiting inheritance confirms the spiritual condition of the adult child registering the objection. The bottom line is that the decisions we make with regard to distributing God's wealth at death should be based on the principles laid out in His word and our accountability to Him, not our concern about the possibility of our adult kids objecting to our decisions.

Next Steps

For those who intend to review their estate plans in light of this discussion and consider making revisions accordingly, here are a few thoughts. While I'm hopeful this book will be useful in rethinking your wealth transfer decisions, I have to recognize the limitations of this format. This study may well have raised more questions than it answered. While the underlying principles are the same for all of us, each family has its own unique set of circumstances. This is where the implementation plan must be tailored to each individual family. How do I progress from simply embracing these foundational estate planning principles to creating a customized wealth transfer plan that makes sense for my family's unique situation?

The first step is to continue searching the Scriptures for additional wisdom on wealth and inheritance. Scripture is replete with passages dealing with money and material possessions. Study passages that relate to every financial concept you can think of – money and possessions, greed and covetousness, giving and generosity, wealth and inheritance, to name just a few. Your best source of wisdom, as you consider how to apply these principles to your family's situation, is God's word. He promises to provide the wisdom we seek (James 1:5).

The second important step is directly related and should be done in conjunction with our study of God's word: prayer. Prayer is an indispensable part of the Christian life in general – how much more so when we're making major decisions with God's resources? Just as Jesus' life modeled the importance of time alone with the Father, so should ours. Before making final decisions with regard to your revised estate plan, be sure to spend a season in Bible study and prayer.

Third and finally, don't hesitate to seek counsel from biblically wise and spiritually mature friends and advisors. This discussion is much too important to go it alone. *Victory is won through many advisors* (Proverbs 11:14b). Don't hesitate to avail yourself of the godly counselors around you.

My Hope and Prayer

I had a strange thought as I was bringing this book to a conclusion. I've always marveled at Christian teachers whose written works continue to bless and instruct God's people generations after they were written. I would guess that most Bible teachers would love to produce such a work – not because of a desire for fame or fortune, but because of a deep desire to have such impact for God's kingdom.

I'm now realizing that if God's people are still reading this book in the 22nd century, I will have failed miserably in my purpose for writing it. My objective is to encourage, exhort and implore this generation of Christians to apply these principles to our wealth transfer plans so we can finish the work God has given us to do. He's given us the money – more than enough – along with His written instructions. If God chooses to answer my prayers with regard to this book, within a couple of generations, it will no longer be needed.

What If We Get This Wrong?

The thought that has haunted me since I began this study is this: What happens if we get it wrong? What if we fail to incorporate God's principles of inheritance into our estate plans, whether through ignorance or disobedience? If we're to believe the research cited in prior chapters, the result will be tragic. Five trillion dollars of God's money, excess resources entrusted by Him to this generation to accomplish His purposes, will be passed down and likely squandered by a generation ill-equipped to receive it. A generation of adults, many of which grew up in Christian homes, but whose lives show little evidence of commitment to Christ – and many more who have blatantly rejected the faith altogether – will be made independently wealthy by Christian parents who failed to heed God's instructions.

The percentage of Christians in America is small and declining. Research indicates that the next generation of Christians is considerably less likely to share our commitment to Christ's church, giving generously or completing the Great Commission. In fact, there is also a waning commitment to long-held evangelical truths such as the inerrancy of Scripture, God's ownership of all resources and the Lordship of Jesus Christ. Barring a significant revival, which God can surely bring at any time He chooses, our generation is much more likely to faithfully steward this excess wealth than the next.

If we get this wrong, it is entirely possible this significant amount of wealth God has entrusted to us will be passed down and squandered. The best-case scenario would simply be the next two generations having been made independently wealthy and never having the opportunity to rely on God. The worst-case scenario is that countless lives and families will be destroyed by our having provided the resources needed to fund highly consumptive lifestyles, remove the consequences of persistent financial irresponsibility and exacerbate existing addictions. A lot of damage can be done with $5 trillion dollars.

What If We Get This Right?

What if, on the other hand, we get this right and make the most of this incredible opportunity? What if we are willing to commit at least a healthy portion of this excess $5 trillion to finishing the work in our generation? The world will be forever changed by our obedience. Every city, town and village not yet reached will hear the Gospel proclaimed. Every people group without access to God's written word in their heart language will be provided Bibles of their own. In short, if we are faithful in our stewardship of the resources God has entrusted to us, the Gospel will be preached, and disciples made, among every nation, tribe and language. This Gospel of the kingdom will have been preached to the ends of the earth as a testimony to all nations, just as Jesus promised (Matthew 24:14).

And then, Lord willing, the end will come. "Amen, come Lord Jesus" (Rev 22:20).

END NOTES

Introduction

1. Giving USA: 2015 Was America's Most-Generous Year Ever, Published: June 13, 2016.

Chapter 7

1. The Great Evangelical Recession by John Dickerson. Copyright 2013. Published by Baker Books.
2. The Great Evangelical Recession, page 29.
3. "Has Everyone Heard?" JoshuaProject.net
4. Christian Aid Mission (christianaid.org)

Chapter 8

1. The Great Evangelical Recession (pages 84-85)
2. The Great Evangelical Recession (page 90)